Charles Jackson, Society Providence Franklin

Report on the Geology of Rhode Island

Charles Jackson, Society Providence Franklin

Report on the Geology of Rhode Island

ISBN/EAN: 9783744732550

Printed in Europe, USA, Canada, Australia, Japan

Cover: Foto ©ninafisch / pixelio.de

More available books at **www.hansebooks.com**

PROVIDENCE FRANKLIN SOCIETY.

REPORT

ON THE

GEOLOGY

OF

RHODE ISLAND.

(THREE PLATES.)

PROVIDENCE:
PUBLISHED BY THE SOCIETY.
1887.

ERRATA.

Page 15. Insert "County" after "Bristol," second line above the foot-note.

Page 57. "1877" should read "1887".

Plates II. and III. "X" should be "×".

Page 82. The interrogation mark should be omitted after "*Smoky Quartz*", and inserted after "*Rose Quartz*".

REPORT

OF THE

Committee on the Geology of Rhode Island,

PRESENTED TO THE

PROVIDENCE FRANKLIN SOCIETY,

IN 1887.

Your committee, appointed June 19, 1883, has held various meetings and presented to the Society partial and verbal reports. Permission was given, January 6, 1885, to report in print; but other engagements have heretofore prevented the completion of the work.

It has been found advisable to divide the report into the following distinct portions :—

I. Index of Publications bearing upon the Geology and Mineralogy of Rhode Island.

II. Catalogue of Rocks and Minerals collected during the Geological Survey of Rhode Island, in 1839.

III. Catalogue of Fossils found in Rhode Island.

IV. Catalogue of Minerals found in Rhode Island.

V. List of Localities in Rhode Island of interest to the geologist and mineralogist.

VI. Results obtained by digging and boring in Rhode Island.

VII. General Remarks.

The following list, arranged under the first of these heads, is not presented as one that is entirely complete. It is merely a sition" (now Carboniferous). "Transition rocks extend from R. I. to Boston," p. 639. Anthracite coal of R. I., p. 410.

1818. AMOS EATON. "Index to the Geology of the Northern States." Several editions were published in subsequent years, with different titles; and in 1830 and 1832 it appeared as a " Geological Text Book." New York.

1819. I. W. WEBSTER. *American Journal of Science*, vol. 1, pp. 243–4. Asbestos in the Anthracite from R. I. Refers to Dr. Meade's account of R. I. coal.

1822. THOMAS H. WEBB. *Amer. Journ. Science*, vol. 4. Fluor Spar near Providence, R. I., p. 50. Notice of 10 minerals in the vicinity of Prov., R. I., pp. 284–5. Notice of localities of 6 minerals in R. I, including Titanium and Cyanite, " an uncommonly beautiful mineral," vol. 5, pp. 402–3.

1822. GEORGE T. BOWEN. *Amer. Journ. Science*, vol. 5. Nephrite from Smithfield, R. I. So called by Dr. Meade, but doubt expressed whether it is genuine nephrite. " This beautiful mineral is of a lively apple green." Specimen furnished to Prof. Silliman by Mr. Bowen, of Providence. [Since called Bowenite.] p. 39. Also "Vegetable Impressions of ferns and other plants remarkably distinct in transition slate, Providence, R. I.," p. 42. Analysis of the above variety of Nephrite by George T. Bowen, of Prov., in laboratory of Yale College. " Its color is bright apple green — sometimes tinged with blue." Differs from nephrite in chemical composition — more water and very little alumina — also infusible before blowpipe and inferior in hardness. Like nephrite in other respects. pp. 346–348.

1823. BENJAMIN SILLIMAN. *Amer. Journ. Science*, vol. 6, p. 353. Fusion of Rhode Island anthracite.

1823. G. TROOST. *Journal of the Academy of Natural Sciences of Philadelphia*, vol. 3, pp. 222–3. Notice of the Yenite of Rhode Island. First time found in United States, at Cumberland, R. I., 15 miles north of Providence. Description given, sometimes called lievrite (also ilvaite.)

1823. JOHN TORREY. *Annals of the Lyceum of Natural History of N. Y.*, vol. 1, p. 51. Notice of a locality of Yenite in the United States. Description given. Specimen from Samuel Eddy, of Prov., R. I., found at Cumberland.

1824. G. TROOST. *Transactions of the American Philosophical Society*, held at Philadelphia, for Promoting Useful Knowledge, vol. 2, pp. 478–480. " Notice of a New Crystalline Form of the Yenite of R. I." Described, with colors, location, etc.; called by Troost, " Prismatic Yenite." Specimen furnished by Dr. Robinson.

1824. THOMAS H. WEBB. *Amer. Journ. Science*, vol. 7. New locality of Fluor Spar, in Cumberland, R. I., purple, blue, green, and white, p. 54. Three Rocking Stones near Providence, and one in Foster, R. I., p. 61.

1824. STEUBEN TAYLOR. *Amer. Journ. Science*, vol. 7. " Notice of a Rocking Stone in Warwick, R. I." " The Drum Rock," at Apponaug, with full description and plate, a full page drawing, by Moses Partridge, pp. 201–203. Ferruginous sand at Block Island, and Green Talc at Smithfield, R. I., p. 254.

1824. CHARLES U. SHEPARD. *Amer. Journ. Science*, vol. 7, p. 251. Yenite in Cumberland, R. I., at Tower Hill, with description.

1824. J. ADAMS. *Amer. Journ. Science*, vol. 8, p. 199. Amethysts and other minerals lately found in Bristol, R. I.

1824. STEUBEN TAYLOR, THOS. H. WEBB, and SAMUEL ROBINSON. *Amer. Journ. Science*, vol. 8, pp. 225–232. Localities of R. I. minerals, including the Yenite of Cumberland, Amethyst of Bristol and Cumberland, Zoisite and sulphuret of Molybdena, with magnetic oxide of Iron, in Cumberland; and many other minerals, in various towns of the State.

1825. " N." *Amer. Journ. Science*, vol. 9, pp. 28–39. " On Bowlders and Rolled Stones." Ocean the cause, has retired from the land, perhaps water gone into caverns in the earth, p. 34. Refers to Newport for power of ocean, pp. 28–9.

1825. J. G. and J. B. ANTHONY and SAMUEL ROBINSON. *Amer. Journ. Science*, vol. 9, pp. 46, 47, 49–53, 401. The Anthonys furnish localities of 17 minerals and impressions on shale from R. I. Robinson furnishes localities of 10 minerals, including Yenite; and 50 rock specimens from R. I., including basalt in mica slate, magnetic iron stone of Cumberland, gray wacke, etc. Good description of Purgatory conglomerate, near Newport.

Prof. Silliman acknowledges the receipt from the Franklin Society of very fine specimens of the Bristol Amethyst. One piece was cut, polished, and set in gold, to be worn as a bosom pin, presented to Prof. S. by the Providence Franklin Society. It is commended as bearing "an advantageous comparison with the finest foreign specimens." It was ground and set by Davis and Babbitt; but the work was first incorrectly attributed to George Baker.

1825. SAMUEL ROBINSON. "A Catalogue of American Minerals, with their Localities; including all which are known to exist in the United States and British Provinces." 316 pp. Boston. Pages 79–91 and 290 are devoted to R. I., with 21 towns represented. Five pages are given to Cumberland minerals. Most of the minerals of R. I. appear in this book,— though not all with modern names,— including Amethyst, Yenite, Zoisite, Nephrite, etc. "Smithfield. Basalt? about a mile northwest from Woonsocket village in the race-way of the Branch cotton mill, in walls or veins, imbedded in mica slate, consisting of columns of various sizes and figures, their faces corresponding to each other so as to form a compact wall."

1825. LARDNER VANUXEM. *Journ. Acad. Nat. Sciences of Phila.*, vol. 5, pp. 17–27. "Experiments on Anthracite, Plumbago, etc." Analysis of R. I. anthracite, pp. 20, 21. Also in *Amer. Journ. Science*, 1826, vol. 10, pp. 102–109, followed by replies of Hare and Silliman.

1825. "An Address to the Inhabitants of Rhode Island on the subject of their Coal Mines." New York, 16 pp. Dated at Newport.

1826. OWEN MASON. *Amer. Journ. Science*, vol. 10, pp. 9–11. Notice of two Rocking Stones in R. I., with two drawings: Fig. 1, N. Prov.; Fig. 2, Smithfield. Localities of Epidote, Fibrous and Glassy Tremolite, Fetid Quartz, and Actynolite, in R. I.

1826. SAMUEL ROBINSON. *Amer. Journ. Science*, vol. 10, pp. 225–227. Nacrite, Brown Spar, and Actynolite, in R. I.

1826. BENJAMIN SILLIMAN. *Amer. Journ. Science*. Anthracite Coal in Penn., with notes on R. I. coal, vol. 10, pp. 332–3, 336–7, 342, 344.

Anthracite Coal of R. I.—remarks upon its properties and economical uses — read before the Conn. Academy of Arts and Sciences, vol. 11, pp. 78–100.

1827. WILLIAM MEADE. *Amer. Journ. Science*, vol. 12. Remarks on the Anthracites of Europe and America, with special references to R. I. coal, pp. 75–83. Also Epidote in R. I., p. 309.

1829. AMOS EATON. *Amer. Journ. Science*, vol. 16, pp. 299–301. "Argillite, embracing Anthracite Coal," in R. I. and elsewhere. The facts were supposed to answer the question, "Have we such a rock as primitive argillite?" At that time there was discussion whether there are both a primitive and a transition argillite, or the latter only.

1829–37. *Manufacturers and Farmers' Journal*, Providence. Articles on R. I. Coal, Jan. 5 and 15, 1829; March 17, 1831; Jan. 15, 1835; April 25 and October 17, 1836; April 13 (structure of Prospect Hill) and Oct. 26, 1837.

1830. CHARLES U. SHEPARD. *Amer. Journ. Science*, vol. 17, pp. 142–144. The new species, "Ferro-silicate of Manganese," found by him in Cumberland, R. I., at the same time, and in the same rock, with Yenite; and at first considered identical with it. Ferro-silicate of Manganese first found by Dr. Thomson, in a specimen from N. J., and first described by him in *Annals of the Lyceum of Natural History of N. Y.*, vol. 3, p. 28.

1830. W. W. MATHER. *Amer. Journ. Science*, vol. 18, p. 360. Iron sand, Carnelian, Jasper, "a chlorite," and iron pyrites, found at Westerly and Fort Adams.

1832. CHARLES UPHAM SHEPARD. "Treatise on Mineralogy." New Haven. Second edition, 1844, 168 pp.

1837. CHARLES U. SHEPARD. "A Report on the Geological Survey of Conn." 188 pp. New Haven. Confined chiefly to Mineralogy. 1. An Economical Report. 2. A Scientific Report. 3. A Descriptive Catalogue of the cabinet of about 600 samples collected.

1837. JAMES D. DANA. "A System of Mineralogy." New Haven, 580 pp. Revised editions were published in '44, '50, '54. The 5th edition, 1868, New York, 827 pp.; Appendix 1, '68–'72; Ap. 2, '72–'75; Ap. 3, '75–82; by G. J. Brush and E. S. Dana.

1837–39. CHARLES T. JACKSON. "Geology of the State of Maine." Three Annual Reports, printed by the State. Also Two Annual Reports on the Geology of the Public Lands belonging jointly to the States of Mass. and Me.

1837–47. LOUIS AGASSIZ. Various articles and books upon glaciers and the glacier theory, mostly in the French language.

1838. "A Report of the Important Hearing on the memorial of the New England Coal Mining Company for encouragement from the State; and on the Numerous Petitions of the Freeholders in aid of the same; before the Select Special Committee of the General Assembly of Rhode Island and Providence Plantations; Together with the Report of the Committee unanimously adopted by the Assembly in favor of the Prayer of the Memorialists and Petitioners, and of a Geological and Agricultural Survey of the State in 1838." New England. 148 pp.

1840. CHARLES T. JACKSON. "Report on the Geological and Agricultural Survey of the State of Rhode-Island, made under a Resolve of Legislature in the Year 1839." 312 pp. Providence.

This contains fourteen wood-cut illustrations in the text, seven plates in distinct pages, four colored sections, and a geological map of the State, also colored for the formations. It is the only geological work devoted exclusively to Rhode Island and covering the whole State. The General Assembly appropriated $2000, and the Society for the Encouragement of Domestic Industry $500, to defray the expenses of the survey. The time devoted to the work was one year.

Considerably less than one-half of the whole number of pages is devoted to geology proper, the remainder of the report treating of the origin of soils, agricultural statistics, agricultural observations on the Island of Rhode Island, the chemical analysis of soils, and farm reports. The report of the commission of 1876 calls this survey a "reconnoisance." It was by no means full and exact when published, and the changes in geological theories and nomenclature within the last half century have been so great, that this book is practically nearly obsolete, and needs to be interpreted to the present generation. The necessity for a new survey is apparent, and it is to be hoped that the United States and the State government will soon supply the want.

Any one studying the geology of Rhode Island will, of course, consult Jackson's report, so that no full summary need be given here. The whole western half of the State, the northern, the southeastern, and most of the extreme southern part of the State are colored on the map as "Primary." The region about Narragansett Bay, running N. E. into Mass., is "Transition Grau-wacke." Block Island and a strip from Warwick to Pawtucket are "Tertiary." The Primary rocks are granite, gneiss, and mica slate. Granite Jackson considers certainly, and gneiss probably, of igneous origin; but mica slate is a primary stratified rock which "has stronger claims to a metamorphic origin." The "Hornblende Rock," of Cumberland, Smithfield, and Johnston he considers "decidedly a rock of igneous origin, like the greenstone trap rocks," though it sometimes "presents the appearance of regular stratification," which he attributes to the admixture of the fused rock with argillaceous slate. Narrow strips of rock between the Transition and Primary are marked as "Metamorphic." As Jackson considered the Primary rock of igneous origin, it is evident that he supposed its heat had modified the adjoining Transition sedimentary rock in all cases. Grau-wacke or graywacke is a conglomerate containing pebbles of small size united by an argillaceous cement. It is generally of a gray color.

1841. BENJAMIN SILLIMAN, JR. *Amer. Journ. Science*, vol. 40, pp. 182–194. Review of Dr. Jackson's Report on Geol. & Agr. Survey of R. I. Prof. S. discusses the Purgatory conglomerate near Newport, speaks of minute crystals of magnetic iron on pebbles and in cement; states, with Jackson, that the fissure 8 to 10 ft. wide and 36 to 44 ft. deep "was once occupied by a trap dyke, most of which has been washed away by the sea." Does not accept Jackson's theory that gneiss is "the mere crust of rapidly cooled granite." Predicts that the names Cambrian and Silurian "will be found to be convenient appellatives for vast regions of our country, subordinate to the more extensive class of transition," notwithstanding Jackson prefers the Wernerian division of transition rocks to the terms Cambrian and Silurian.

1841. EDWARD HITCHCOCK. "Final Report on the Geology of Massachusetts,"* 2 v., 831 pp., 55 plates. Northampton.

Worcester anthracite coal older than that of R. I., and not connected with it, p. 127. Anthracite coal of R. I., pp. 129–138; Cumberland and Newport, p. 135, Portsmouth, p. 136.

Granite of Fort Adams from Fall River (Troy), Mass., p. 148. Graywacke quarried in Pawtucket and on Conanicut Island, p. 180.

Cumberland magnetic iron ore, p. 195; copper ore, p. 204. Boulders of Cumberland magnetic iron transported south 35 miles; also other boulders in Little Compton, Tiverton, etc., p. 380. "Diluvial Grooves" in Newport, p. 386 and map, plate 53. Boulder near junction of Taunton and Fall rivers, of coarse graywacke conglomerate, 40 or 50 ft. in diameter,

---

*Mass. ordered a survey in 1830. An Annual Report of 70 pp. was published in 1832, and another of 700 pages in 1833. A new survey was ordered, and another annual report of 139 pp. was published in 1838, the final one as above, of 831 pp. and 55 plates.

covered by 10 ft. of drift, and worn and scratched on the top of the boulder, pp. 373, 393-4.

"Graywacke," "Coal Measures," and "Old Red Sandstone" of Mass. and R. I., pp. 531–545. These pages include first suggestion that R. I. coal is of carboniferous age (see also pp. 137, 138); discussion of conglomerate with elongated nodules at Purgatory, near Newport, island of R. I. (fig. 108) (also pp. 296, 297); strike and dip of strata in Pawtucket, Cumberland, Providence, Portsmouth, Warren, Seekonk, Newport, Bristol, Tiverton, and Little Compton; fossils named. See also, Map of dip and strike, Plate 53; Geolog. Map, Plate 52; Section F, Plate 55.

"Metamorphic Slates" of Mass. and R. I., pp. 546–554. Newport, with sketch, fig. 109, p. 550; "Quartzose Aggregates" at Purgatory; "Mica Slate" in Wickford, Smithfield, and Cumberland; "Amphibolic Aggregate" of S. E. island R. I. (pp. 535, 548); "Flinty slate," "Jasper," etc., of Newport; "Zoisite" in Middletown; iron and copper in Cumberland, p. 554.

Minerals found in limestone of Smithfield, p. 565. Why limestone dolomitic at Smithfield and Newport, pp. 582–584. Strike and dip of "hornblende slate" in Cumberland and Smithfield, p. 623; of gneiss in Burrillville, Smithfield, and Little Compton, p. 635. Granite in Little Compton, Tiverton, Portsmouth, and Bristol, p. 681 and geol. map plate 52. Vein of feldspar with fault, in granite, Newport, p. 693, fig. 178. Amethyst of Bristol from Mt. Hope granite, p. 700. Suspected anticlinal axis in R. I., p. 708.

Where N. W. & S. E. system of strike intersects N. E. & S. W. system in N. E. corner of R. I. is one of the most metalliferous spots in New England; former system (N. W. & S. E.) more extensive in R. I. than Mass., p. 713, map plate 53.

Hitchcock gives the catalogue numbers of 63 specimens of rock formations from R. I. in the Mass. State collection, as follows: From Smithfield 18, Cumberland 16, Newport 12, Middletown 5, Pawtucket 4, Little Compton 3, Portsmouth 2, Bristol 1, Warwick 1, Wickford 1. These include 14 specimens of the "graywacke" formation (including coal), from Cumberland, Pawtucket, Newport, Portsmouth, and Middletown; 12 of the "metamorphic slates," from Newport, Middletown, Wickford, and Smithfield; 9 of the "talcose slate," from Smithfield, Cumberland, and Little Compton; 6 of the "hornblende slate," from Smithfield and Little Compton; 6 of limestone, from Smithfield and Newport; 5 of granite from Cumberland, Smithfield, and Bristol; 4 of quartz rock from Cumberland; 3 of mica slate, from Cumberland, Smithfield, and Warwick; 2 of serpentine and 1 of "porphyry" from Newport; 1 of syenite from Cumberland. The minerals masonite and zoisite are also included in the R. I. specimens.

1841. CHARLES T. JACKSON. *Amer. Journ. Science*, vol. 41. Remarks on joints in Purgatory conglomerate, R. I., p. 172; and on "phenomena of diluvial currents" in R. I., boulders of porphyritic titaniferous iron transported southward from Cumberland, p. 176. In Report of Second Annual Meeting of Assoc. of Amer. Geologists.

Also in *Transactions* of that association, pp. 25, 28. Cumberland iron found on a tract 40 miles N. to S. and from 6 to 15 miles in width, diverging to the S. In 1842 Jackson opposed glacial theory as taught by Agassiz, p. 46.

1841. EDWARD HITCHCOCK. *Amer. Journ. Science*, vol. 41, pp. 232–275. "Address before the Association of American Geologists." List of State Geological Surveys. Dolomitic limestone usually found in regions of great disturbance, theory of sublimation from interior of earth probable, p. 240. Discusses favorably glacier theory, then attracting attention on account of the publication of the works of Agassiz.

1841. WALTER R. JOHNSON. *Proceedings of the Academy of Natural Sciences of Philadelphia*, vol. 1, pp. 118, 119. Remarks on samples of Anthracite from R. I. Coal of same age as that of Penn., but subjected to high temperature and intense pressure. Fossils prove age, coal formerly thought more ancient.

1842. JAMES G. PERCIVAL. "Report on the Geology of the State of Connecticut," with Geological Map. 495 pp. New Haven.

A granitic (gneiss) formation (primary) extends from E. Haven nearly parallel with the Sound to Ct. river, then northerly and then easterly to Lantern Hill, then northerly parallel with W. coast of Narragansett Bay to N. E. corner of Ct. This formation presents a high ridge or escarpment on boundary N. and W., bordered immediately in that direction by a well marked valley or plain, pp. 149–152.

Rocks of R. I. border, pp. 157–162 and 177–194. General course of drift S. S. E., sometimes deflected to S. S. W. by local obstructions. Many examples of boulders transported, scratches, etc.

1842. EDWARD HITCHCOCK. *Transactions Assoc. Amer. Geologists and Naturalists*, pp. 164–221. "The Phenomena of Drift, or Glacio-Aqueous Action in North America, between the Tertiary and Alluvial Periods." Discusses transported boulders, smoothed, polished and striated rocks, valleys of erosion, moraines, terraces, etc.; also three theories of drift: 1. Iceberg theory of Lyell. 2. Elevation of regions round pole precipitating ice and water of northern ocean over countries further S., theory of De la Beche. 3. Glacier theory of Agassiz. Is not ready to accept any one of these unmodified, but believes in "glacio-aqueous" origin of drift. Note, p. 218, states that his address before the association in 1841 was misunderstood as accepting the glacier theory in full.

1843. WILLIAM W. MATHER. "Natural History of New York, Part IV., Geology." (Inside title, "Geology of New York, Part I., Geology of First Geological District.") 653 pp., 46 plates. Atmospheric causes producing boulders by disintegration seen in Foster, R. I., trappean rocks, pp. 163–4. Block Island once connected with Long Island, pp. 30, 161. Boulders from R. I. on L. I., pp. 166, 167, 171. The peculiar "round-backed hillocks with bowl-shaped cavities or valleys between them," "composed of boulders, rounded pebbles, gravel and sand," form an elevated ridge which is the "backbone" of the island, and once extended, perhaps, to Plum, Gull, and Fisher's islands. It separates into two ranges at Smithtown, half-way the length of Long Island, and one extends through the south branch of L. I. to Montauk Point, and probably once to Block Island, as the eastern end of L. I. was once much larger than at present. Reefs of loose blocks of rock, and fishing ground for tautog between Montauk Pt. and Block Island and along S. shore mentioned as evidence. The main feature of the topography of L. I. is the range of hills from W. to E., occupying most of the northern half, with a nearly level plain, slightly undulating, extending from S. base of hills to S. shore. Valleys from heads of bays on N. shore cross the plain to S. shore, as though made by currents of water, p. 271.

1844. CHARLES T. JACKSON. " Final Report on the Geology and Mineralogy of the State of New Hampshire, with Contributions towards the Improvement of Agriculture and Metallurgy." 384 pp., 11 plates. Concord.

1845. F. ALGER. *Amer. Journ. Science*, vol. 48, pp. 218, 219. " Formula of the Masonite of Dr. Jackson," with reference to Alger's edition of Phillips's Mineralogy, p. 132.

1845. CHARLES LYELL. *Quarterly Journal of the Geological Society of London*, vol. 1, pp. 199-202. " On the probable Age and Origin of a Bed of Plumbago and Anthracite occuring in mica-schist near Worcester, Mass." Quotes Jackson and Hitchcock, refers to red sandstone of Attleboro' as probably Devonian; anthracite of R. I. and impure plumbago of Worcester probably of same age as coal of Penn.

Also a Geological Map of U. S. and Canada in 1845 and in 1855, accompanying " Travels in N. Amer."

1845-48. CHARLES B. ADAMS. Four Annual Reports on the Geology of Vermont.

1846. J. E. TESCHEMACHER. *Boston Journal of Natural History*, vol. 5, pp. 370-385, plates 33-36. " On the Fossil Vegetation of America." R. I. species figured.

1848. JAMES D. DANA. " Manual of Mineralogy." New

Haven, 430 pp. Revised in 1857. The third edition, 1878, New York, 474 pp., has " and Lithology " added to the title.

1849. EDWARD HITCHCOCK. *Proceedings of the American Association for the Advancement of Science*, vol. 2, pp. 148–156. "On the River Terraces of the Conn. Valley, and on the Erosions of the Earth's Surface." Two Purgatories in R. I., p. 153.

1849. J. D. WHITNEY. *Proceedings of the Boston Society of Natural History*, vol. 3, pp. 100–102. "Composition of Chloritoid or Chlorite-spar, and Masonite." Suggests retaining name Masonite for hydrous chloritoid. Also in *Amer. Journ. Science*,* vol. 8, pp. 272–3.

1849. *Mfg. and Farm. Journal*, Providence. Articles on R. I. Coal, Jan. 11, Jan. 18, July 26, Nov. 26, Dec. 17.

1850. CHARLES T. JACKSON. *Proc. Amer. Assoc. Adv. Science*, vol. 4, pp. 188–190. "On Ancient Pot-holes in Rocks."

1851. J. LAWRENCE SMITH. *Amer. Journ. Science*, vol. 11, p. 64. Masonite of R. I.

1852. R. HERMANN. *Amer. Journ. Science*, vol. 14, p. 269. Masonite.

1852. I. R. BARBOUR. "Coal Beds of Rhode Island. Mount Hope Coal Mine." New York, 24 pp. This pamphlet contains Dr. Jackson's special report on that mine, and refers to reports of A. A. Hayes and J. T. Hodge.

1853. J. LAWRENCE SMITH AND GEORGE J. BRUSH. *Amer. Journ. Science*, vol. 15, p. 212. Bowenite of R. I. identical with Serpentine.

1853. EDWARD HITCHCOCK. Report to the Governor of Mass. on certain points in the Geology of Mass., with map of Bristol, and R. I. coal-field. State document, Boston. Extract below.

---

* The number of the Series can be determined by the date. The Second Series of the *Amer. Journ. Science*, commonly called *Silliman's Journal*, began in 1846; and the Third Series in 1871.

1853. EDWARD HITCHCOCK. *Amer. Journ. Science*, vol. 16, pp. 327–336. "The Coal Field of Bristol Co. and of R. I." Extract from report last named. In 1840, Pres. Hitchcock suggested that part of this region, previously considered more ancient, might be of Carboniferous age; now he advances a step further, and declares the whole tract Carboniferous. Bristol Co., a part of Plymouth Co., the whole of the island of R. I., and a strip on the W. side of Nar. Bay, a tract "embracing not less than 500 square miles, is a genuine coal-field, that has experienced more than usual metamorphic action," mechanical and chemical. This coal formation is of the same age as the coal deposits of Penn., Va., Ohio, Mich., Ill., and Iowa; England, Scotland, France, and Belgium. The following reasons are given:—

I. "The general outline of the surface over this field, corresponds with that of a regular coal field, or basin."

II. "The rocks correspond essentially to those of the coal measures." 1. Dark colored slate in immediate contact with the coal, especially beneath it. 2. A coarse light gray grit immediately above the coal bed. 3. A dark gray, hard grit between the beds of coal. 4. Coarse gray conglomerate probably underlying the other rocks and perhaps the equivalent of the "millstone grit" of other coal fields. Age of the rock on the borders of this coal field uncertain. Red slates and sandstones, probably Devonian, rise in the S. part of Wrentham 400 feet above the surface at the Mansfield coal mines and pass beneath the coal field.

III. "The number, position, strike, dip, and general character of the beds of coal, already discovered in the district under consideration, render it probable that it is all one coal field, or essentially one." Details of coal found in Mass., Cumberland, Valley Falls, Seekonk, Providence, Cranston, Bristol, Portsmouth (Case's mine and Aquidneck mine) and Newport.

IV. "The character of the vegetable remains found in connection with these coal beds, makes it almost certain that they belong to the coal measures of the carboniferous system." Names of certain fossils are given.

1853. Jules Marcou. " Geological map of the U. S. and the British Provinces of North America," with text and sections. Also map in Peterman's Journal in 1855, again in 1858, etc.

1853–4. Edward Hitchcock. " Outline of the Geology of the Globe, and of the United States in particular." 136 pp., with 2 maps. R. I., with exception of " coal measures " in the N. E., is colored as " hypozoic and metamorphic rocks, with granite, syenite and porphyry."

1854. R. C. Taylor and S. S. Haldeman. " Statistics of Coal: including mineral bituminous substances employed in Arts and Manufactures; with their geographical, geological, and commercial distribution and amount of production and consumption on the Amer. continent." Second edition, Philadelphia. Rhode Island, pp. 446–456. Localities of coal, largely from Jackson and Hitchcock. Quotes Vanuxem on quality of R. I. anthracite and Emmons on the " Taconic system." Fig. 16, " Transverse Section of the Portsmouth Anthracite Basin, R. I., looking N. ;" also a second Portsm. section described. Is disposed to consider R. I. coal metamorphic, and of the same age as that of Penn., of " secondary " origin; though its character, except for fossils, might readily lead geologists to ally the series to " transition " or " primary " rocks.

1854–5. Ebenezer Emmons. " American Geology." Author of the " Taconic system ; " geologist of one district of N. Y., also of N. C.

1856. Henry D. Rogers. Geological Map of U. S. and British N. Amer., published in A. Keith Johnston's Physical Atlas. Edinb. and London. R. I. mostly " metamorphic, gneiss, mica slate, etc. ;" but some igneous granitic rocks represented, also carboniferous.

1857. Edward Hitchcock. " Smithsonian Contributions to Knowledge," vol. 9, art. 3. " Illustrations of Surface Geology." 164 pages and 12 plates. 1. On Surface Geology, especially that of the Conn. Valley, in New England. 2. On the Erosion of the Earth's Surface, especially by Rivers. 3. Traces of Ancient Glaciers in Mass. and Vt.

1860. EDWARD HITCHCOCK. *Proc. Boston Soc. Nat. Hist.*, vol. 7. Elongated, flattened, and curved pebbles found in conglomerate of Vt. and Newport, R. I. Pres. Hitchcock's theory of plastic state presented by his son, E. H., Jr., pp. 208-9, and by himself, pp. 353-4. Objections stated by Dr. C. T. Jackson: smoothness and absence of indentation show no change, wave action advocated.

1860. WILLIAM B. ROGERS. *Proc. Boston Soc. Nat. Hist.*, vol. 7. Presented to the Society, in the name of Norman Easton, of Fall River, a mass of siliceous slate containing the imprints of shells, and gave an account of the discovery of these fossils in some of the pebbles of the conglomerate of that region, pp. 389-391. Prof. R. visited the neighborhood with Mr. E., and found the fossils both in loose pebbles and in the conglomerate in Dighton. Fossils probably of two species, resembling *Lingula prima* and *L. antiqua*, of the Potsdam sandstone. Parent rock of the pebbles unknown. Fossils also found in Newport conglom., p. 392.

"On the Causes which gave rise to the Generally Elongated Form and Parallel Arrangement of the Pebbles in the Newport Conglomerate." pp. 391-393. Ascribes cause to wave and current action. Objections to Prof. Hitchcock's view: 1. Cleavage planes run in wrong direction. 2. Lingulae fossils not distorted. 3. Some pebbles not elongated. Account in *Amer. Journ. Science*, 1861, vol. 31, pp. 440-442.

1860. WM. B. ROGERS. *Proc. Amer. Assoc. Adv. Science*, vol. 14, p. 227. "On the Recent Discovery, by Mr. Norman Easton, of Fossils in the Conglomerate of Taunton River." Published only by title.

1860. CHARLES H. HITCHCOCK. Geological Map of Aquidneck, or the Island of R. I. Presented by the City of Newport to members of the Amer. Association for the Advancement of Science, at the Newport meeting.

1860. CHARLES H. HITCHCOCK. *Proc. Amer. Assoc. Adv. Science*, vol. 14.

"Geology of the Island of Aquidneck," pp. 112-137. Rocks as follows, beginning with the oldest: 1. Talcose schists and conglomerates, 1,000 ft. thick, at Sachuest Point, probably older than Carboniferous. 2. Conglomerate at Purgatory, Paradise, etc., 500 ft. thick, with description and figures of pebbles which must have been distorted and elongated since deposition, while rock was plastic through heat; joints perfectly smooth, as if glazed rather than polished by friction, rock not moved since; perhaps age of millstone grit or subcarbonifcrous; similar conglomerates in Tiverton, Dighton, Warwick, Cranston, Providence, etc. 3. Schists and Slates W. of Purgatory, 473 ft. thick. 4. Second Conglomerate, on Easton's Point, pebbles rarely distorted, 464 ft. thick. 5. Coal Measures, 3588 ft. thick, composing most of the island, consisting of dark slate, anthracite and plumbago, green slate, grits and sandstones, and conglomerates; list of fossil plants; coal mines of Portsmouth. 6. Third Conglomerate, 50 ft. thick, with small masses of anthracite among pebbles, proving it later than coal measures, Miantonomah Hill, Coaster's Harbor Island, and S. part of Newport. 7. Metamorphic Rocks, 1,321 ft. thick, including siliceous slate, chert, jasper, serpentine, and dolomitic limestone, Newport Neck. 8. Granite and Protogine (chloritic), 100 ft. thick, some fragments of slate imbedded in the granite, S. part of Newport and the Dumplings; either igneous in origin, or produced by aqueo-igneous fusion of Carboniferous rocks, at close of Paleozoic. 9. Alluvium, 50 ft. thick, mostly unmodified drift, large boulders, Cumb. iron ore, etc., striae about S. Section at S. end of island, p. 119. Tables of thickness, strike, and dip of all strata observed. Granite at extreme N. end of island probably Huronian or Laurentian, p. 133.

" Synchronism of Coal-Beds in the New England and Western United States Coal-Basins," pp. 138–143. Lists of about 30 fossil plants found in Wrentham, Mass., Valley Falls, Portsmouth, and Newport, examined by Leo Lesquereux, and from them exact age of coal strata determined; all are lower coal measures; doubtful whether upper coal measures are to be found in New Eng. Whole Carboniferous system in Newport 6,497 ft. thick, including Nos. 2–8 Geol. Is. Aquid. Eleven different seams of coal in N. part of Portsmouth. Quotations from Lesquereux comparing R. I. coal field with those in Nova Scotia, Penn., and the West, of same age.

1861. T. STERRY HUNT. *Amer. Journ. Science*, vol. 31, pp. 392–414. "On some points in American Geology." 1. Laurentian system, the oldest strata of the earth's crust, found in the Laurentide and Adirondack mountains, etc., consisting of gneiss, quartzite, some conglomerate, limestone, dolomite, serpentine, plumbago, iron ores, basic feldspars without quartz and with more or less pyroxene, but no argillites and talcose and chloritic schists. 2. Huronian system, consisting of quartzites, conglomerate, limestones, peculiar slaty rocks, and diorite, which are regarded as altered sediments. 3. Appalachian crystalline strata, consisting of feldspathic gneiss, quartzites, argillites, micaceous, epidotic, talcose and specular schists, with steatite, diorites, etc., which Hall, Logan, and Hunt, regard as altered paleozoic sediments, while H. D. Rogers regards them as older than paleozoic.

Hunt argues from the iron ore, metallic sulphurets, and graphite, the presence of vegetation, and from apatite and silicified forms the presence of animal life, even in the Laurentian, p. 396. He considers that the character and composition of sediment indicates the age of the rock, even the crystalline strata of different ages having different chemical and lithological character. "The gradual removal of alkalies from aluminous rocks has led to the formation of argillites, chloritic and epidotic rocks, at the same time removing carbonic acid from the atmosphere, while the resulting carbonate of soda by decomposing the calcareous and magnesian salts of the ocean, furnished the carbonates for the formation of limestones and dolomites, at the same time generating sea salt," p. 395. Hunt's views on these points and on the nature and formation of silicates, the relation of metamorphism and pseudomorphism, etc., are presented in the *Amer. Journ. of Science* at various times from 1857 to 1860: vol. 23, pp. 437–8; vol. 24, pp. 272–3; vol. 25, pp. 102–3, 287–289, 435–437, 445; vol. 26, pp. 109–10; vol. 28, pp. 170–187, 365–383 (a statement of his views on the formation of gypsums and magnesian rocks, continued in vol. 42, pp. 49–67); vol. 30, pp. 133–137.

Also in the reports of the Geological Survey of Canada, and other publications, especially his "Essays," 1874.

1861. EDWARD HITCHCOCK. "Report on the Geology of Vermont," published by Albert D. Hagar, under the authority of the State Legislature. 2 vols., 988 pages, Claremont, N. H. Discussion of Newport, R. I., and other similar conglomerate, pp. 28-44. Pebbles drawn out while plastic, and joints caused by some *polar* force (not mechanical), such as heat or galvanism. In this he answers the objections of Prof. Rogers and Dr. Jackson.

1861. EDWARD HITCHCOCK. *Amer. Journ. Science*, vol. 31, pp. 372-392. "On the Conversion of certain Conglomerates into Talcose and Micaceous Schists and Gneiss by the Elongation, Flattening and Metamorphosis of the Pebbles and the Cement." Same as Vt. Report, above.

1861. E. HOLMES AND C. H. HITCHCOCK. Sixth Annual Report of the Secretary of the Board of Agriculture of the State of Maine, 464 pp. Newport Conglomerate, p. 178. Also 1862-3, Second Annual Report upon the Natural History and Geology of the State of Maine, 447 pp.

1862. JAMES D. DANA. "Manual of Geology." Philadelphia, 798 pp. Revised in 1874, New York, 828 pp. In the earlier editions of his map, the Carboniferous of R. I. extends towards Worcester in Mass.; in the later it turns towards Boston. In the earlier editions of his works the area of R. I. and Mass. coal measures is given as 1,000 square miles; in the later, 500 miles. In all his editions, R. I. is given as of undetermined age, with the exception of the carboniferous.

1863. JAMES D. DANA. "A Text-book of Geology." Philadelphia, 354 pp. Revised in 1874, 1877, and 1883. Fourth Edition, New York, 412 pp.

1864. WILLIAM E. LOGAN. "Geological Map of Canada and the adjacent region," including the Northern United States, accompanying "Geological Survey of Canada." More than half of his " Carte géologique du Canada," 1855, is of the U. S. Other editions were published in 1866, '68, etc.

1865. A. S. PACKARD, JR. *Memoirs Boston Soc. Nat. Hist.*, vol. 1, pp. 210-262. " Observations on the Glacial Phenomena of Labrador and Maine."

1866. N. S. SHALER. *Proc. Boston Soc. Nat. Hist.*, vol. 10, pp. 358-364. " On the Formation of the Excavated Lake Basins of New England." Ice melting beneath the glacier from an outflow of internal heat a cause of eroding basins.

1866. BENJAMIN S. LYMAN. *Proc. Amer. Assoc. Adv. Science*, vol. 15, p. 83. "Against the Supposed Former Plasticity of the Puddingstone Pebbles of Purgatory, R. I."

1867. CHARLES WHITTLESEY. *Proc. Amer. Assoc. Adv. Science*, vol. 16, pp. 92-97. " Depression of the Ocean during the Ice Period." Water of ocean lessened by formation of ice on land; earth's crust sank under thickest ice and rose elsewhere.

1867. CHARLES H. HITCHCOCK. *Proc. Amer. Assoc. Adv. Science*, vol. 16, pp. 124-127. " The Distortion and Metamorphosis of Pebbles in Conglomerates."

1868. GEORGE L. VOSE. *Mem. Boston Soc. Nat. Hist.*, vol. 1, pp. 482-487. " On the Distortion of Pebbles in Conglomerates, with Illustrations from Rangely Lake, in Maine." Plates 17-19. Hard and rigid pebbles " bent and flattened, without becoming what would be called plastic"; result of severe compression continued for a long time, developing heat enough for chemical changes.

1869. WILLIAM P. BLAKE. *Proc. Amer. Assoc. Adv. Science*, vol. 18, pp. 199-205. " The Plasticity of Pebbles and Rocks." Result of mechanical force alone, without a very high temperature.

1868. THOMAS S. RIDGEWAY. " Memorial in relation to the Coal-field of R. I., Presented to the General Assembly," Jan., 1868; with Supplement, Feb., 1870. 12 pp., Providence. Original pamphlet 9 pp., dated 1867. Mr. R. was for three years supt. of Pocassett Coal and Iron Co., mine in Cranston. Urges manufacture of iron from R. I. ore, using R. I. coal. Latter contains carbon 80 per cent., silica 10, alumina 6, lime and magnesia 3. No sulphur in the mass, though it is sometimes found in the interstices, where it would be immediately dissipated when thrown on fire.

1869. R. I. SOCIETY FOR THE ENCOURAGEMENT OF DOMESTIC INDUSTRY. Report on Coal and Iron in R. I., with extracts from Providence Journal, letters by R. H. Thurston and others. 16 pp., Providence. History of mining iron and coal in R. I. Two millions of tons Cumberland iron ore above drainage; also hematite in Cranston, bog ores and iron sand in other towns. The Cumb. ore is " ilmenite," or " titaniferous magnetic ore," specially valuable as a " steel ore," containing 2 per cent. oxide manganese and 10 per cent. oxide titanium, besides silica, magnesia, alumina, etc.; but is free from sulphur or phosphorus. Anthracite, some of which yields 90 per cent. of carbon, is abundant, also free from sulphur and phosphorus, and the best coal known for smelting iron. Description of Portsmouth coal mines.

1870. N. S. SHALER. *Proc. Boston Soc. Nat. Hist.*, vol. 13. " On the Parallel Ridges of Glacial Drift in Eastern Mass., with some Remarks on the Glacial Period," pp. 196–204. Allusions to Long Island, Cape Cod, etc. Terminal moraine of earlier glacial time far out to sea, and to it we owe the formation of the broad submerged table land which borders the northern coast of U. S., p. 203. " Note on the Glacial Moraines of the Charles River Valley, near Watertown," pp. 277–279. " W. H. Niles thought that there were certain features in the topography and surface-geology of the region spoken of which it would be difficult to reconcile with a terminal moraine located as described by Prof. Shaler," p. 280.

1870. T. STERRY HUNT. *Proc. Boston Soc. Nat. Hist.*, vol. 14, pp. 45–49. " On the Geology of the Vicinity of Boston." Refers to rocks occurring " with dolomite and massive dark colored serpentines in the city of Newport, R. I., where the beds have also a high dip to the N. W.," as belonging to a second division of " crystalline stratified rocks."

"These ancient rocks are in various places penetrated by intrusive granites, which are generally more or less hornblendic — the syenites of Hitchcock and others. They often contain true feldspars, as in the well-marked granite of Newport, which there cuts the greenish dioritic and sometimes amygdaloidal rocks," p. 46.

1870. T. STERRY HUNT. *Amer. Journ. Science*, vol. 50, pp. 83–90. "On the Geology of Eastern New England." Proposes to call the White Mt. series "Terranovan" [Newfoundland], above the Laurentian. Formerly referred to Devonian, but now separated as crystalline, distinct from Laurentian, Labradorian, and Huronian. Same in *Canadian Naturalist*, vol. 5, pp. 198–205.

1870–78. *Providence Journal.* Articles on Coal, Jan. 6, '70; June 17, '71; Jan. 11, '76; April 20, '78.

1871. T. STERRY HUNT. *American Naturalist*, vol. 5, pp. 450–509. Address on retiring from the office of President of the Amer. Assoc. for the Advancement of Science. "The Geognosy of the Appalachians and the Origin of Crystalline Rocks." Division of crystalline strata by lithological characteristics into three series, of different ages: 1. Adirondack (or Laurentian). 2. Green Mountain (or Huronian). 3. White Mountain (or Montalban). The Labradorian (or Norian) system is spoken of as upper Laurentian or pre-Huronian, found in the Adirondack region, but not certainly known in the Appalachian range. Although, in common with most other American geologists, Hunt had previously considered the crystalline rocks of the Green and White Mountain series to be altered paleozoic sediments, he now concludes that all the "crystalline schists of eastern North America are not only pre-Silurian but pre-Cambrian in age."

Allusion to some Newport, R. I., strata as of 2d series (Huronian), p. 460. Dolomitic or magnesian limestones not formed by the alteration of pure limestones, but by direct sedimentation, chemical precipitation from solution, pp. 504–508.

This address is also published in vol. 20 of the *Proceedings of the Association* for 1871, pp. 3–59.

Notice of the same address, with adverse criticism, is found in *Amer. Journ. Science*, vol. 2, pp. 205–207.

1871. JAMES D. DANA. *Amer. Journ. Science*, vol. 1, pp. 1–5, 125–6. "On the Quaternary, or Post Tertiary, of the New Haven Region." "The Glacial era an era of Glaciers, and not of Icebergs."

Vol. 2. "On the Connecticut River valley Glacier, and other examples of Glacier movement along the valleys of New England," pp. 233–243, 305. "On the position and height of the elevated Plateau in which the Glacier of New England, in the Glacial era, had its origin," pp. 324–330. Dana, by the direction of the scratches, locates the head of the New Eng. glacier on the water-shed between the St. Lawrence and Hudson bay, the high ridge running N. E. & S. W. between Lakes Temiscamang and Mistissinny, thus giving the southeasterly movement of the ice over New England. See also "Note on the Glacial era," vol. 13, pp. 79, 80.

1872. N. S. SHALER. *Amer. Naturalist*, vol. 6. "On the Geology of the Island of Aquidneck and the neighboring parts of the shores of Narragansett Bay," with Plate 6, containing 3 sections across the Bay. (Extracts from a Report to Prof. Benj. Peirce, Supt. of the U. S. Coast Survey.)

General Topography, pp. 518–528. Nar. Bay "the southernmost point of the fiord structure on our coast." Transverse and longitudinal sections of the bay show its channels to be broad but relatively shallow excavations, with a gradual slope seaward. The valleys of the island, which run N. and S., are glacial amplifications of original valleys of erosion made by streams of water; the same is true of the great valleys which now form the Bay. The channels E. and W. of the island were probably "occupied by distinct glacial streams for a short period towards the close of the last ice time." Depressions in drift, generally with rudely circular outlines, usually not over 100 feet across and 20 feet in depth, probably caused by "gaps in the ice on the surface of the glacier," made by streams. Ponds of the island are similar glacial depressions on a larger scale. The topography of the island does not express the structure of the underlying rock; and this fact is a strong indication of the action of ice. General absence of sand in the beaches about the island indicates want of recent great movements of the land which would furnish much material for the sea to work over, while there are no currents to bring sand from Cape Cod shore or Long Island. "In recognizing the harbors and inlets of Nar. Bay as glacial work, we get an example of the agent which has given nine-tenths of the havens of our sea-boards."

Glacial Deposits and Ice Marks, pp. 611–621. Drift of the island mostly of local origin, transported a short distance towards the south. Débris on the island deposited by the melting of a mass of ice (continental glacier) in which it was held; not deposited as terminal moraines, except at two points. Instances of "shock and lee sides" and "roches moutonnées;" work of the ice at Paradise Rocks; abundance, origin, and deposit of surface boulders; rapid and steady retreat of the ice; scratches on the rocks, etc. Probably several glacial periods in the earth's history; channels which separate the island from the main land probably excavated by ice in a glacial period anterior to that " which gave way to make our present time."

Physical Conditions of the Carboniferous Time, pp. 751–760. At the time when the carboniferous beds were formed, "the shore at this part of the continent was not far from its present position," as proved by conglomerate with water-worn pebbles. Fragments of Lingulæ found in pebbles of this formation, "not known to occur in any rocks to the northward nearer than the Champlain region;" but most probably "the source of supply of these fossils has long since been destroyed by erosion," and it may have been located in the immediate neighborhood when these conglomerates were formed. The conglomerates of the coal period prove "that the surface of the country was then made up of syenites, porphyries, felsites, argillites, and related rocks, much as at the present day." "Within the regions where these pebbles were formed, there were no rocks of Silurian or Devonian age, else their evident fossils would have been preserved as well as the lingulæ in the pebbles of the conglomerate." "The work of metamorphism which has so much affected the character of the rocks of this region was already done at this the beginning of the coal period." The coal conglomerate probably the result of glacial action which preceded the carboniferous age and prepared the earth's surface for the growth of coal plants. Compression of the pebbles.

1872. JOHN B. PERRY. *Proc. Boston Soc. Nat. Hist.*, vol. 15, pp. 48-148. "Hints towards the Post-Tertiary History of New England, from Personal Study of the Rocks, with Strictures on Dana's 'Geology of the New Haven Region.'" Perry advocates Agassiz's theory of glaciers as opposed to Lyell's theory of icebergs. Refers to Dana's paper read before Conn. Academy of Arts and Sciences, which also appeared in separate form. Opposes Dana's idea of glaciers in valleys moving in different directions from the great continental glacier above them, and urges theory of local glaciers at commencement and close of period to account for different marks and transportation of boulders. Thinks there was, during glacial period, no elevation of land, as Prof. Dana urges, but possibly a depression of the ocean. Most of this paper was read in 1870, abstract published, vol. 14, pp. 62-3.

1872. U. S. COAST SURVEY. Topography of Narragansett Bay. Transfers from Plane Table Sheets. Scale $\frac{1}{10000}$. Sheet No. 21.

1873. U. S. COAST SURVEY. Chart of Narragansett Bay. Scale $\frac{1}{10000}$. Contour lines every 20 ft. difference of level. Sheet No. 353.

1873. A. S. PACKARD. *Amer. Naturalist*, vol. 7, pp. 210-213. "Comparison of the Glacial Phenomena of New England with those of Europe."

1873. JAMES D. DANA. *Amer. Journ. Science*, vol. 5, pp. 198-211, 217. "On the Glacial and Champlain eras in New England." The New Eng. glacier probably extended 60 or 90 miles S. of Long Island. "In the Glacial era, the land over the higher latitudes probably stood *above* its present level," as shown by fiords; but in the Champlain *below*, as shown by the height of sea-border terraces. Fiords are cited as evidence of the former, though they " may have been begun long before the Glacial era, in earlier periods of elevation," and they may have been finished before the Glacial era. The absence of Cretaceous and Tertiary deposits along the American coast N. of Cape Cod shows the land to have been higher to the north in those periods. "There are no true *lateral* moraines of the Glacial era in N. Eng.; for the glacier was not a valley glacier, but one of continental character, although far from covering the whole continent." There may have been a few local ones formed during the decline of the glacier in the Champlain era. "No distinct *terminal* moraines of the Glacial era have been observed in New England." Long Island drift suggests a terminal moraine; but it was probably the work of the Champlain era, or that of melting.

1873. JAMES D. DANA. *Proc. Amer. Assoc. Adv. Science*, vol. 22, B., pp. 25–27. " On Staurolite Crystals and Green Mountain Gneisses of the Silurian Age." Presence of Staurolite no evidence of pre-silurian age. Also same in *Amer. Naturalist*, vol. 7, pp. 658–660; and *Canadian Naturalist*, vol. 7, p. 163.

1873. ELIAS LEWIS. *Popular Science Monthly*, vol. 2, p. 634. "Bowlder-like masses of clay in the Long Island drift."

1874. THOMAS STERRY HUNT. " Chemical and Geological Essays." Boston, 489 pp.

1874. CHARLES H. HITCHCOCK and WILLIAM P. BLAKE. " Statistical Atlas of the U. S. based on the results of the Ninth Census, 1870, with Contributions from many eminent men of science and several Departments of the Government, compiled under authority of Congress by Francis A. Walker, Supt. of the 9th Census." Map of the Coal Fields of the U. S. N. Eng. Basin, including coal measures in Mass. & R. I., 750 square miles. Coal " plumbaginous anthracite." Details from *Proc. Amer. Assoc.* for 1860. Also Geological Map of the United States and Territories. Eozoic and Metamorphic rocks cover most of R. I.; Carboniferous as usual, E. and N. E. part; Silurian in N. W. part of R. I.

These authors also prepared in 1876 a Geological Map of the U. S. to accompany the Smithsonian report for the Centennial; and Hitchcock one in 1878 for Gray's Atlas, Phila.

1874. N. S. SHALER. *Memoirs Boston Soc. Nat. Hist.*, vol. 2, pp. 321–340. "Preliminary Report on the recent Changes of Level on the Coast of Maine: with reference to their origin and relation to other similar changes." Weight of ice cause of depression of land in glacial period, p. 322.

1874–78. CHARLES H. HITCHCOCK. "The Geology of New Hampshire. A Report comprising the Results of Explorations ordered by the Legislature." 5 Parts in 3 Vols. Concord.

Vol. 1. Part I. Physical Geography, 668 pp.

Vol. 2. Part II. Stratigraphical Geology, 684 pp. Geological Map of New England with portions of the adjacent states and provinces, plate I., p. 8. "The territory includes what might be termed the 'Champlain island,' or that portion of the continent east of the Hudson valley which existed as an isolated district for a long time after the Glacial period," p. 7. The "Gulf of Maine" appears on this map, and submarine banks of less than 300 feet depth. The western part of R. I. is given as "Atlantic" (Montalban); the northeastern, Huronian; and the eastern, Carboniferous. Possibly rocks associated with serpentine and dolomite at Newport, R. I., belong to Huronian, p. 12. Quotes from his papers of 1860 on Carboniferous rocks of R. I., but with these differences: "First coarse conglomerate, with distorted pebbles, 300 ft." (instead of 500); "coal measures, 3,500 ft." (instead of 3,588); total, 4787 ft. (omitting Nos. 1, 7, 8, and 9). Hitchcock divides the Eozoic, or Archean, rocks into Laurentian, Montalban, Labradorian, and Huronian. He drops the word "Atlantic" and uses Montalban in its place; but makes it underlie Huronian, while Dr. Hunt makes it overlie the same. Pp. 8–12, 669, 674, 675.

Vol. 3. Part III. Surface Geology, 386 pp., comprises "Modified Drift" (by WARREN UPHAM) and "Glacial Drift," with Appendices; and is an exhaustive treatment of the subject, with thorough discussion of till, kames, plains, terraces, boulders, striae, etc. Terminal moraine S. of New Eng., pp. 300-305. Part IV. Mineralogy and Lithology, 262 pp. (by GEO. W. HAWES), contains a full description of 95 minerals found in the State, and of all rocks not simple minerals; with 12 plates of microscopic sections, finely executed, many of them beautifully colored, as viewed by polarized light. Part V. Economic Geology, 104 pp.

1874. "Report of the State Board of Education on the Proposed Survey of the Commonwealth" of Massachusetts, 19 pp. This includes the report of a special committee, Benj. Peirce, T. Sterry Hunt, N. S. Shaler, and Sam. H. Scudder. House Doc. Nos. 40 and 184, 1875, contain the above, remarks and letters by various "scientific and other gentlemen," memorials from scientific societies, a bill for a survey, etc. The survey was not made, however, at that time, nor in accordance with that plan.

1875. J. D. WHITNEY. "Geographical and Geological Surveys," 96 pp. Cambridge. From *N. Amer. Review.*

1875. W. W. DODGE. *Proc. Boston Soc. Nat. Hist.*, vol. 17, pp. 388-419. "Notes on the Geology of Eastern Mass." Magnesian limestone in crystallines, with nephrite, at Smithfield, R. I., p. 393. Slates at Sachuest Point, Newport, Portsmouth, Little Compton, etc., p. 399. Newport conglomerate, pp. 411-2. Norfolk Co. Basin, pp. 412-414.

1875. N. S. SHALER. *Proc. Boston Soc. Nat. Hist.*, vol. 17, pp. 488-490. "Note on the Geological Relations of Boston and Narragansett Bays." Great faulted down-folds, imprisoning within the lower crystalline rocks a great thickness of Paleozoic strata. "To this protection we owe the preservation of a great thickness of the rocks between Cambrian and the Upper Carboniferous, which have been lost over the surface where they were exposed to the intense erosion of the successive glacial periods that swept this shore." "Ridges of the height of thousands of feet have lost their relief since the Carboniferous period, while the similar ridges of the Alleghanies have not been anything like as much eroded,"—more severe here because repeatedly subjected to glacial wearing.

Vol. 18, pp. 126–133. "Propositions concerning the Motion of Continental Glaciers." Ice melting below 32° F. by pressure of weight a cause of eroding basins.

1875. WM. B. ROGERS. *Proc. Boston Soc. Nat. Hist.*, vol. 18, pp. 97–101. "On the Newport Conglomerate." Re-iterates the views expressed by him in 1860 in opposition to Pres. Hitchcock's theory of plasticity. Speaks of making a tracing of the conglomerate surface at Purgatory on transparent cloth, giving outlines of pebbles with direction of laminae in each. Says the chasm at Purgatory "has been erroneously regarded as due to the decay of a dyke of trap, supposed to have occupied the cavity." Has recently found impressions of Lingulae in Newport conglomerate suggestive of those found many years ago near Fall River.

This article also appeared as pp. 3–7 of "Geological Notes," 13 pp. Boston, 1875.

1875. JAMES D. DANA. *Amer. Journ. Science*, vol. 9, pp. 223–4. Presence of iron ores and apatite in Archean not sure evidence of life.

Vol. 10. "On Southern New England during the Melting of the great Glacier." I. "The Flood from the melting Glacier," pp. 169–183. II. "Absence of marine life from Long Island Sound through the Glacial and part of the Champlain periods," pp. 280–282. III. "Reindeers in Southern New England," bones found in glacial clay, near New Haven, Ct., pp. 353–357.

IV. "Depression of the land, or amount of subsequent elevation," pp. 409–438. An important mark of stratified "river-valley, estuary, or sea-border formations consists in the total or nearly total absence of great bowlders from their level surface," though the bowlders may abound on the slopes of the adjoining hills. Between Watch Hill and Point Judith bowlders are found down to within 11 ft. of high water level, but not lower. An examination is made of five valleys of Southern New England, the last of which is Narragansett Bay. The terrace at Providence on which a part of the city is built is 80 ft. above high water; that at East Greenwich is 56 ft.; the meadows near the ocean, 11 ft.

"No marine relics have yet been found in Champlain deposits about any part of Narragansett Bay to mark the sea-level. Such fossils should be looked for with more care than has hitherto been used; but much looking will probably end in finding none. The great glacier must have filled the channels among the islands; and as the ice disappeared, the floods, having a strong pitch owing to the height at Providence, would have made a profound sweep through them. Absence of marine fossils is therefore what should reasonably be expected."

Certain pre-glacial stratified sand-hills, easily mistaken for drift formations, are found along the shores between Watch Hill and Point Judith. Block Island, Long Island, and other islands south of N. Eng. are made up to a great extent of unconsolidated pre-glacial beds, probably Tertiary, in some places upturned and folded.

Dana concludes that the amount of depression in Southern New England during the melting of the glacier was only about 15 feet; that the river valley formations are not marine; and that the height of the flood was the chief cause of the height of the terraces. After making allowance for 15 ft. difference of level at Point Judith, and 1 to $1\frac{1}{2}$ ft. per mile for increase of depression northward, the pitch of the stream during the flood at Providence was only 1 to $1\frac{1}{2}$ ft. per mile, though it was as high as 8 ft. per mile in one of the other valleys studied.

"Supplement: The Overflows of the flooded Connecticut," pp. 497-508.

1876. JAMES D. DANA. *Amer. Journ. Science.* "On the Damming of Streams by drift ice during the melting of the great Glacier," vol. 11, pp. 178-180. Appendix: "On the discharge of the flooded Mill River into the Quinnipiac, and the effects as registered in the drift deposits of the New Haven plain," vol. 12, pp. 125-128.

1876. JAMES T. GARDNER. "Uses of a Topographical Survey to the State of New York. A Report to the Amer. Geographical Society." 14 pp., New York.

1876. MESSAGE OF GOV. LIPPITT to the R. I. General Assembly. Approves the plan of the Commission for a new survey of the State.

1876. "Report of the Commission to prepare a Plan for a thorough Geological and Scientific Survey of the State." Presented to the General Assembly of Rhode Island at its January Session. 13 pp., Providence. The commission, two of whom were to be nominated by the Providence Franklin Society, consisted of Zachariah Allen, Wm. F. Channing, George I. Chace, John R. Leslie, and George F. Wilson. They recommended the appointment of a Board to have permanent charge of the survey; the appropriation of $20,000 for the geographical survey, in four annual installments of $5,000 each; the publication of a map; a subsequent geological survey; to be followed by a compilation of the natural history of the State. This plan was not carried out.

1876. U. S. COAST SURVEY. "Coast Chart No. 13. Cuttyhunk to Block Island, including Narragansett Bay." Scale $\frac{1}{80000}$. Sheet No. 113.

1876. L. S. BURBANK. *Proc. Boston Soc. Nat. Hist.*, vol. 18, pp. 224–5. "Remarks on the Conglomerate of Harvard, Mass." Specimens exhibited showing "a gradual transition from a nearly unaltered conglomerate to a crystalline gneissoid rock." Remarkable examples of flattened and curved pebbles found.

1876. GEORGE FREDERICK WRIGHT. *Proc. Boston Soc. Nat. Hist.*, vol. 19, pp. 47–63. "Some Remarkable Gravel Ridges in the Merrimack Valley." Quotes Clarence King on origin of kames in Rocky Mts., and King's observations upon Naushon (one of the Eliz. Is.), "unquestionably a part of a terminal moraine." "The arrangement of the ridges of boulders, with their convexities always to the S., or away from the source of supply, together with the characteristic conical depressions, left me in no doubt as to the origin of the island," pp. 62–3. Martha's Vineyard "based upon inclined tertiary clays," covered with a confused mass of terminal rubbish, but no true moraine ridges.

1876. CHARLES H. HITCHCOCK. *Proc. Boston Soc. Nat. Hist.*, vol. 19, pp. 63–67. "Lenticular Hills of Glacial Drift." Cape Cod, Eliz. and Long Is., pp. 66–7.

1876. WARREN UPHAM. *Proc. Amer. Assoc. Adv. Science*, vol. 25, pp. 216–225. "On the Origin of Kames or Eskers in New Hampshire."

1877. A. L. HOLLEY. *Transactions of the Amer. Institute of Mining Engineers*, vol. 6, pp. 224–227. "Notes on the Iron Ore and Anthracite Coal of R. I. and Mass." Gives analysis of Portsmouth and Cranston coal, Cumberland magnetite and Cranston hematite. Iron manufactured in R. I. in 1703. Cannon cast in Revolution and 1812.

1877. S. T. LIVERMORE. "A History of Block Island." 371 pp. Hartford, Conn. Surface very uneven, no even hill-sides nor level plains. "Imagine several tidal waves moving in nearly the same direction — from W. to E., each rising about 150 ft. above the level of the sea, and their bases nearly touching each other; and on the tops, sides, and intervals of these, 'chop-waves' in every conceivable shape and position covering completely the tidal waves; and when the reader has done this he has an outline of the view under the observer's eye who stands in a good light upon Beacon Hill." Originally the surface "was wellnigh paved with small bowlders." More than 300 miles of stone-wall now. No ledge yet discovered on the island; but bowlders large enough to be blasted for walls. Stones rounded, "granite with hardly an exception." Soil "has no lime apparently." "Its basis is sand and gravel, with a few spots of valuable clay." Acres of black iron sand along the bathing beach and between Harbor Pond and the sea, pp. 20–23, 162, 168.

Much of the surface formerly covered with a heavy growth of timber. Inexhaustible stores of peat in the valleys, made from vegetable matter washed down little hill-sides into ponds. Three beds extend into the ocean. One bed traced from high-water mark one quarter of a mile out into the sea, and peat brought away that burned well, pp. 21–29, 156. Soft coal found, pp. 30, 155.

Over 100 ponds, varying in size "from the duck pool to the Great Pond, which is said to cover 1,000 acres." The Great Pond has a maximum depth of 12 fathoms, on the W. side, nearest the sea, from which it is separated by a narrow strip of land; water supplied from the sea, freshened by filtering through sand; formerly connected with sea by a creek. No ponds sustained by springs or streams; some supplied with fresh water by sea, as above, others, on higher ground, have clay bottoms, holding surface water; one of them, Sands' Pond, 100 feet above the sea, fed from some unknown source, pp. 156–163.

Sandy Hill, base $\frac{1}{4}$ mile N. to S. $\frac{1}{8}$ mile E. to W., rising 100 ft. to a point, a pile of drift (sand and gravel), mostly destitute of vegetation. "Its base rests upon a bed of peat, which shows that it was thrown up after the island had produced vegetation." Beacon Hill the highest land on the island, about 300 feet high. The Bathing Beach anciently had sandy banks 25 ft. high, so steep as to be hard to climb; sand banks carried away to the sea by strong winds of winter, making the beach. Black iron sand left there because too heavy to be blown into the sea, pp. 164–168.

Clay Head, on the Neck, conspicuous for its high bluffs, three kinds of clay, blue, red, and white. Native coral has been found on the E. and W. shores of the island. Island rapidly diminishing in some places; some portions sinking. The Hummuck was a peninsula on the extremity of Sandy Point, the extreme N. end of the Neck; an elevation of land on which small trees and bushes grew, washed away long ago, leaving the Point as a sand bar, pp. 174–5.

1877. EDWARD S. DANA. "A Text-Book of Mineralogy, with an extended Treatise on Crystallography and Physical Mineralogy." New York. Revised in 1883; with Appendices A, B, C, D, E, 537 pp.

1877. ELIAS LEWIS, JR. *Popular Science Monthly*, vol. 10, pp. 434–446. "Ups and Downs of the Long Island Coast." L. I. a terminal glacier moraine.

Amer. Journ. Science, vol. 13. Water Courses and Valleys upon Long Island, pp. 142–146. Plains S. part of island.

Thirty shallow valleys in 50 miles, running W. of S. Due to motion of earth on its axis? pp. 215–6. Heights on L. I., pp. 235–6.

1877. WARREN UPHAM. *Amer. Naturalist*, vol. 11, pp. 524–539. " Surface Geology of the Merrimac Valley." Drift and glacial action, dunes, kames, etc.

Amer. Journ. Science, vol. 14, pp. 459–470. " The Northern Part of the Conn. Valley in the Champlain and Terrace Periods." Explains nature and origin of kames as in New Hampshire Report —" shown by their position to be the oldest of our modified drift deposits."

1877. WILLIAM O. CROSBY. *Amer. Naturalist*, vol. 11, pp. 577–587. "Notes on the Surface Geology of Eastern Mass." Drift and glacial action. Water and nature of the rocks more effective than ice in shaping topography. Most of the fiords are older than Post-tertiary.

1877–80. GEORGE H. COOK. Annual Reports of the State Geologist of New Jersey. Tracing the terminal moraines from L. I. across N. J. by Cook and Smock.

1878. T. STERRY HUNT. " Second Geological Survey of Penn. E. Special Report on the Trap Dykes and Azoic Rocks of Southeastern Penn. Part 1. Historical Introduction." Harrisburg, 253 pages. Full history of investigations concerning these ancient crystalline rocks of Canada, New England, and Appalachian region, with quotations from previous works, being a "History of American Pre-Silurian Geology," with some acct. of Cambrian. Newport Huronian rocks, pp. 189–191. Present arrangement: 1. Laurentian. 2. Norian (Labradorian, or Upper Laurentian). 3. Huronian (Green Mt. series). 4. Montalban (White Mt., or Mica-schist series). 5. Taconian. 6. Keweenian. 7. Cambrian. 8. Siluro-Cambrian. Montalban and Taconian together once called Terranovan by Hunt.

1879. T. STERRY HUNT. *Proc. Amer. Assoc. Adv. Science*, vol. 28, pp. 279–296. " The History of some pre-Cambrian Rocks in America and Europe." He opposes the two common theories : 1. That these crystalline rocks are of plutonic (igneous) origin. 2. That they are metamorphosed paleozoic or later rocks. He asserts: "1. All gneisses, petrosilexes, hornblendic and micaceous schists, olivines, serpentines and in fact all silicated crystalline stratified rocks, are of neptunean origin, and are not primarily due to metamorphosis or to metasomatosis either of ordinary aqueous sediments or of volcanic materials. 2. The chemical and mechanical conditions under which these rocks were deposited and crystallized, whether in shallow water or in abyssal depths (where pressure greatly influences chemical affinities), have not been reproduced to any great extent since the beginning of paleozoic time. 3. The eruptive rocks, or at least a large part of them, are softened and displaced portions of these ancient neptunean rocks, of which they retain many of the mineralogical and lithological characters," p. 281.

1879. CHARLES H. HITCHCOCK. *Geological Magazine*, London, p. 248. "The Glacial Period in Eastern America."

1879. GEO. F. WRIGHT. *Proc. Boston Soc. Nat. Hist.*, vol. 20, pp. 210-220. "The Kames and Moraines of New England." Terminal moraine in Block Is. and along S. shore of R. I., p. 216.

1879. WARREN UPHAM. *Proc. Boston Soc. Nat. Hist.*, vol. 20, pp. 220-234. "Glacial Drift in Boston and Vicinity." "Lenticular hills" not found in the terminal moraine of L. Is., etc., p. 232.

1879. WARREN UPHAM. *Amer. Journ. Science*, vol. 18, pp. 81-92 and 197-209. "Terminal Moraines of the North American Ice-sheet." Traces "Extreme Terminal Moraine" and "Second Terminal Moraine" through L. I. and New England, lying 5 to 30 miles apart. The length of the first, or southern, from the W. line of N. J. to Sankaty Head on Nantucket, is about 300 miles, running through Montauk Point, Block Island, No Man's Land, Gay Head and other parts of Martha's Vineyard. The length of the second, or northern, from Port Jefferson to the E. shore of Cape Cod is about 180 miles, running through Orient Point, Plum and Fisher's Is., the southern part of R. I., the Elizabeth Islands, and N. Sandwich, where it turns at a right angle.

Of the unstratified deposits, "the lower till, which seems to be the ground-moraine of the ice-sheet, is very hard and compact, dark and frequently bluish in color, with clayey detritus and its pebbles and bowlders planed and striated; while the upper till, commonly from one to five feet thick, appears to be material which was held in the ice-mass and dropped upon the surface at its melting, being distinguished by its comparative looseness, its yellowish color caused by the exposure of its iron to oxidation, the predominance of gravel and sand instead of clay, and by the abundance and large size of its bowlders, which have seldom been worn or rounded except by the weather," p. 87.

Montauk composed of stratified drift, p. 86. Pre-glacial formations with fossils, overlain by drift, on Gardiner's Island and elsewhere, pp. 89, 90. Height of various hills and ponds on Block Island above sea; kinds of rocks and thickness of layers along S. and N. E. shores of that island, comprising modified drift, upper and lower till. Part of Clay Head seems to be wholly of glacial origin, but another part of it has pre-glacial beds of white and red clay at the base. Lignite found ¼ mile S. from breakwater in lower part of bank 20 to 35 ft. high which forms the shore, in fragments preserving the distinct grain of the wood, and in friable layers. Surface of island also partly modified drift and partly till, both plentifully strewn with bowlders, pp. 91, 92. Further exploration is needed to compare the lignitic beds of Block Is. with the tertiary of Gay Head, the shell bed of Gardiner's Is., and some lower strata of L. Is., p. 90.

The second moraine is well developed in southern R. I. for 17 miles through Westerly, Charlestown, and S. Kingstown, passing into the sea 2 miles W. of Point Judith. "Its whole course may be finely seen from the carriage road in going from Watch Hill through Charlestown and Perryville to Wakefield," the road after the first three miles lying at the S. foot of the hills of the moraine. Chin, Cranberry, Fort, and Village Hills in Westerly; Indian Burying, Sand, "Old Mountain," and Bunker Hills in Charlestown; and Broad Hills in S. Kingstown, belong to this series, some of them stratified and some unmodified, pp. 202-3. " Extensive portions of the terminal moraines were deposited, as we have seen, by rivers which flowed from the surface of the melting ice when a warmer climate returned." "Wherever angles occurred in the terminal front of the ice its surface had converging slopes, which would be likely to produce extraordinary fluvial deposits. This may explain the origin of the thick beds of stratified drift which form nearly the whole of Block Island, and of the plains in S. Kingstown, R. I., which extend six miles N. from the angle of the second moraine, reaching from Tucker's and Worden's Ponds to the N. line of the township," p. 206.

1879. WARREN UPHAM. *Amer. Naturalist*, vol. 13, pp. 489-502 and 552-565. "The Formation of Cape Cod." Two moraines on eastern part of L. I., both with plains to the S. of them. The northern, made up of hills of glacial drift with small areas of level modified drift on S. side, is found along whole extent of L. I., E. of Port Jefferson, is continued in Plum and Fisher's Islands, thence into S. W. corner of R. I., extends 17 miles close to coast of R. I. nearly to Point Judith; about two miles N. W. of P. J. this range sinks to the sea level, probably turns southward into the ocean, and reappears in the Elizabeth Islands, runs N. E. & N. on Cape Cod, then E. into ocean. Southern moraine is continued in Block Island, No Man's Land, part of Martha's Vinyard and Nantucket. Coast of New England bordered by submerged tertiary beds, similar to those above sea level in southern states.

1879. WARREN UPHAM. *Proc. Amer. Assoc. Adv. Science*, vol. 28, pp. 299-310. "The Succession of Glacial Deposits in New Eng." Striæ, p. 300. 1. Lower till or ground moraine, frequently called "hard-pan," usually clayey and dark or bluish in color. 2. Intercalated beds of clay and sand occasionally found. 3. Upper till, deposited at melting. 4. Modified drift, of which kames are the oldest. 5. Plateaus of modified drift, deposited between valleys filled with ice, in a few places. 6. Valley drift, pp. 300-305. Also terminal moraines of L. Is., Block Is., S. part of R. I., etc., as in other papers; lenticular hills of lower till, etc., pp. 305-310. Continuation of ancient N. and S. water-courses below the present sea-level,—bays, ponds, etc.,—on islands and coast of southern New Eng. shows that the ocean did not there "rise so high upon the land in the glacial period as now; though it appears at the same time to have stood above its present height N. from Mass. Bay," p 307.

1879. CHARLES W. PARSONS. "First Annual Report of the State Board of Health of the State of R. I." "Medical Topography of R. I.," pp. 101-111. Geological formation affecting drainage and health, pp. 102-3.

1879, Dec. 2. FREDERICK DENISON. *Providence Journal.* "Glacier Strokes on Mt. Pleasant," Providence. This includes a map of the ledge, with bearings of the different sets of grooves, prepared by the City Engineer of Prov., Oct., 1879. The courses vary from 36° to 17° E. of N., averaging about N. 27° E. magnetic meridian, or N. 16° E. true meridian; hence the glacier is supposed to have moved, on the average, about S. 16° W.

1879. J. MACFARLANE. "An American Geological Railway Guide," giving the geological formation at every railway station, with very small map.

1879. FREDERICK PRIME, JR. *Transactions Amer. Institute Mining Engineers*, Philadelphia, vol. 7. "A Catalogue of Official Reports upon Geological Surveys of the United States and Territories."

1879-84. LEO LESQUEREUX. "Second Geologcial Survey of Pennsylvania. Report of Progress. P." Harrisburg.

"Atlas to the Coal Flora of Penn., and of the Carboniferous Formation throughout the U. S." 87 plates (A, B, I-LXXXV), with explanations.

"Description of the Coal Flora of the Carboniferous Formation in Penn. and throughout the U. S." Vols. I. and II. bound together, 694 pp. and lxiii pp., 2 plates (LXXXVI and LXXXVII.) Description of 23 R. I. species. See "Index B, Habitats," pp. xxxv, xxxvi.

Vol. III. includes text pp. 695–977 and plates LXXXVIII–CXI. Under "Anthracite Basins. Localities of Uncertain Horizon. Rhode Island. Newport and Mount Hope, Coal Mines," is a list of 68 species, pp. 867–8.

1880. U. S. COAST SURVEY. "Eastern Part of Long Island Sound," Point Judith and Block Island to Plum Island. Scale $\frac{1}{80000}$. Sheet No. 114. Second Edition in 1855; edition of 1880 now sold.

1880. GEORGE H. STONE. *Proc. Boston Soc. Nat. Hist.*, vol. 20, pp. 430–469. "The Kames of Maine."
Proc. Amer. Assoc. Adv. Science, vol. 29, pp. 510–519. "The Kames or Eskers of Maine," with map.

1880. G. F. WRIGHT. *Proc. Amer. Assoc. Adv. Science*, vol. 29, p. 426. "An Attempt to estimate approximately the Date of the close of the Glacial Epoch, from an inspection of the Kames and Kettle-holes of New England." Abstract. Full paper in *Amer. Journ. Science*, 1881, vol. 21.

1880. WILLIAM O. CROSBY. "Contributions to the Geology of Eastern Massachusetts." An occasional paper of the Boston Society of Natural History. 286 pp. Boston.

On the geological map are found the northern boundary of R. I. and the extreme northern part of the eastern boundary. The oldest rock appearing on these portions of the boundary between Mass. and R. I. is a small area of *Huronian granite* (hornblendic), of the same age as that at Quincy, near the eastern end of the northern boundary of R. I., N. of Cumberland, pp. 24, 27, 31, 39.

From this Huronian granite west to the Conn. line, embracing nearly the whole of the northern boundary of R. I., is found *Montalban gneiss*. Its dip in R. I. is 30° N. E., p. 136. The strike in N. E. part of R. I., along the Blackstone river, is N. W.– S. E. pp. 9, 129. *Montalban granite* is found at Tiverton, and "cutting the Carboniferous and more ancient slates near Newport, R. I.," pp. 133, 134.

The limestones and "hornblende rock" of Jackson in Cumberland, Smithfield, and Johnston are probably Montalban, though having some characteristics like Huronian, pp. 126–129,

139, 147. Crosby finds in the "hornblende rock" of Jackson fine-grained mica slate approaching argillite; chlorite slate, fine-grained, green and soft; dark-colored, slaty-looking hornblendic rocks; and "other rocks having, frequently a quartzitic, and sometimes a felsitic, appearance." Enclosed in these rocks are the limestones, stratified, frequently magnesian, containing talc and other minerals; also "a rather fine-grained, apparently exotic, granite, hornblendo-micaceous." The strike of these "doubtful beds" of "hornblende rock" is "S. 45°–60° E.; dip, N. E., steep."

The "metamorphic slate" of Hitchcock, a belt of altered rocks traceable southerly as far as Providence or beyond, and overlying the "hornblende rock" and limestones of Jackson, is also Montalban, p. 147. The axis of a well-marked anticlinal extends along the western border of R. I., p. 146. Metamorphic process which changed the conglomerate and elongated the pebbles near Newport, R. I., pp. 148, 230.

"The hard, argillaceous, siliceous, chloritic, and serpentinic slates (the 'flinty slate' of E. Hitchcock) and the associated dolomite, that come between the Montalban granite and Carboniferous argillite on the peninsula of Newport, R. I.," are of about the same age as the "Shawmut group," that is, between the Montalban and the Primordial, pp. 179, 180.

Character of the Narragansett basin, pp. 181–183. Mainly filled with Carboniferous strata; the largest of the three Mass. Paleozoic basins, extending from the western shore of Nar. Bay northeasterly through Bristol and Plymouth counties in Mass., dividing into two branches in Mass. near the N. E. corner of R. I., the northern and narrow branch sweeping first to the N. and then to the N. E. to Braintree, where it nearly, but probably not quite, connects with the Boston basin, as seen on the map. Crosby advances the theory that when the sediments of the Nar. basin were deposited it was an arm of the "Gulf of Maine," expanding and deepening towards the N. E. and having its head towards the S. W., in the vicinity of Newport,—changes in level having taken place "so that what was formerly its head is now open to the sea." See also p. 275.

In the N. E. corner of R. I., running southerly to Central Falls and north-easterly to Braintree, are the supposed Devonian rocks of Pres. Hitchcock, "mainly of a red color, consisting to a large extent of highly ferruginous slate, sandstone, and conglomerate," often grayish or greenish, sometimes with thin layers of limestone and veins of quartz, pp. 273–275, and map.

1880. W. O. CROSBY AND G. H. BARTON. *Amer. Journ. Science*, vol. 20, pp. 416–420. "Extension of the Carboniferous Formation in Mass." "Of the former, if not the present, existence of Cambrian (Lower Silurian) strata in the Narragansett basin there can be but little doubt, since pebbles holding Primordial fossils — *Scolithus* and *Lingula* — are of common occurrence in the conglomerate at Newport, Fall River and Taunton;" and yet this great conglomerate itself is now generally regarded as Carboniferous. The Norfolk Co. beds (including the red rock of Central Falls and Cumberland, the N. E. corner of R. I.) have "been referred by different observers to the Primordial, Devonian, Carboniferous and Triassic systems." The argument for the first is proximity to the Boston basin; for the second and last is the red color. Crosby himself, following Pres. Hitchcock, has heretofore classed them as probably Devonian; but in this article they are shown to be Carboniferous. The Carboniferous beds of the main Narragansett basin consist of (1) conglomerate, sometimes with large boulders; (2) red, gray or green sandstones; (3) coal-measures, black carbonaceous slate, green sandstone and shales. The Norfolk Co. basin contains the first two, but no true coal-measures. This is proved by direct physical connection between the rocks of the two basins, and by fossil *Sigillariae* found in the lowest or conglomerate series in the Nor. Co. basin. These lower beds are the equivalent of the Millstone Grit, and there is no Sub-carboniferous in Mass. and R. I.

1881. GEO. FRED. WRIGHT. *Amer. Journ. Science*, vol. 21, pp. 120–123. "An attempt to calculate approximately the date of the Glacial era in Eastern North America, from the depth of sediment in one of the bowl-shaped depressions abounding in the Moraines and Kames of New England." Pomp's Pond, Andover, Mass. Glacial phenomena of New

Eng. comparatively recent in their origin — not over 10,000 years since. Paper read before Amer. Assoc. Adv. Science, 1880.

1881. M. E. WADSWORTH. *Bulletin of the Museum of Comparative Zoölogy* at Harvard College, in Cambridge, vol. 7, No. 4, pp. 183-187. "A Microscopical Study of the Iron Ore, or Peridotite, of Iron Mine Hill, Cumberland, R. I." Besides magnetite, contains olivine and plagioclase feldspar, with a few irregular flakes of biotite. "The order of crystallization appears to have been, first the magnetite, then the olivine, and lastly the feldspar." Similar to the celebrated iron ore of Taberg, Sweden, which has been worked as an iron ore for over 300 years. Part of the ledge is non-feldspathic, with olivine changed to greenish serpentine, retaining the form of olivine grains. Rock most probably eruptive. Such rocks " give us the most probable clew to the interior composition and structure of the earth." No signs of sedimentation. "The rock nearest to the peridotite is a mica schist some hundred feet away."

1881. JAMES D. DANA. *Amer. Journ. Science,* vol. 22. Quotes from Wadsworth, and says the ore is similar to a chrysolitic magnetite in Orange Co., N. Y., which is metamorphic, and therefore probably R. I. magnetite is also metamorphic, p. 152.

"On the relation of the so-called 'Kames' of the Conn. River Valley to the Terrace-formation," pp. 451-468.

1881. CHARLES H. HITCHCOCK. *Popular Science Monthly,* vol. 20, pp. 229-242. "North America in the Ice Period." Molecular theory of glacier motion, towards the sun, pp. 236-7. Distinctions between upper (ferric) and lower (ferrous) till. Former often very thin, but terminal moraines ferric throughout whole extent, hundreds of feet thick ; terminal moraines S. of New Eng., pp. 238-9. Present submarine channels S. of Cape Cod and L. I. show that the land in the eastern half of N. Amer. was elevated 600 ft. in glacial period, pp. 241-2.

1881. C. H. HITCHCOCK. "Geological Map of the U. S." Scale 20 miles to the inch. Size 13 ft. by 8 ft. New York.

1881, April. CHARLES M. SALISBURY. *Science Advocate*, Atco, N. J. "Geology of the Valley of the Narragansett."

1881. N. S. SHALER and W. M. DAVIS. "Illustrations of the Earth's Surface. Glaciers." 196 pp. and 25 plates. Boston. Excavation of lake basins; shock and lea; boulder trains, Cumberland iron, p. 56. Terminal moraine of old continental glacier through Cape Cod, Martha's Vineyard, Block and Long Islands, pp. 42, 60. Discusses lenticular hills [or drumlins], terraces, kames, etc.; various theories concerning cause of glaciers. Several glacial periods from Cambrian to present time. The last glacial period one of depression of the land, from 20 ft. at southern boundary up to 1,000 ft. in Labrador and 2,000 ft. in Greenland. Hypothesis of Adhémar [ice caps changing center of gravity of earth] has some basis; but that of depressions in earth's crust caused by weight of ice of more value, especially as explaining irregularities in depression. Theories for explaining movement of glaciers. [Shaler.]

List of Works on Glaciers and Glaciation, covering 15 pp. quarto. Plates, mostly photographs of glaciers, moraines, striæ, slickensides, pebbles, weathered boulders, drift sections, lenticular hills, etc., with explanations. [Davis.]

1882. WM. MORRIS DAVIS. *Proc. Boston Soc. Nat. Hist.*, vol. 22, pp. 19–58. "Glacial Erosion." The article is an exhaustive treatment of the subject, with full references to many authorities, and statement of many opinions, often the most contradictory. Traces the growth of the idea of glacial erosion, pp. 21–2. Four lines of argument: A. Action of Glaciers in general. B. Amount and Distribution of Glacial Drift. C. Topography of Glaciated Regions. D. Argument from Necessity.

"In the East, the old surface of the crystalline rocks was generally too rough to allow an equable, non-erosive motion of the ice-sheet; but in the West, the broad, comparatively level country across which the ice advanced, permitted it to pass over loose deposits without seriously disturbing them," p. 40. Drumlins found in intermediate region, between center and margin of glacier. "Glacial erosion was greatest near the centers of glacial dispersion, where the ice acted for the longest time, and where its thickness and velocity were greatest; here it succeeded in scraping away all of the rubbish of pre glacial disintegration and rubbing down the solid rock below in some places for a moderate number of feet; here glaciers lowered the hills and deepened the valleys on which they moved," p. 20. "Most of the solid rock that was carried away came from ledges rather than from valleys; and glaciers had in general a smoothing rather than a roughening effect. In the outer areas on which the ice advanced it only rubbed down the projecting points; here it acted more frequently as a depositing than as an eroding agent. No large lakes have been produced by glacial erosion: the number of true rock-basins of erosion has been greatly exaggerated. The most considerable topographical effect produced by glaciers is the heaping of various morainal deposits on an area smaller than their source, and in this way very often forming hills of considerable size. A similar indirect result of glacial erosion is seen in the very numerous lakes made by drift obstructions in pre glacial valleys."

1882. THOMAS C. CHAMBERLIN. *Third Annual Report of the U. S. Geological Survey,* by J. W. Powell, Director. "Preliminary Paper on the Terminal Moraine of the Second Glacial Epoch," pp. 291–402. Defines the different kinds of till, kames, moraines, etc. "Intermediate or interlobate moraines" are terminal in character but medial in position, "formed by the joint action of two glacial lobes pushing their marginal moraines together, and producing a common one along the line of their contact." Twelve great loops, and several subordinate ones, have been traced in the terminal moraine W. of New Eng., each formed by an ice tongue, or lobe, convex to the south, occupying a pre-glacial valley. The movement of the ice in the center of each lobe was parallel to the axis of the valley, but on the eastern side it diverged gradually to the east, and on the western side to the west.

Moraine on L. I. and New Eng. coast region, pp. 377–381. Prof. C. here follows Upham, but dissents from the view that the two moraines mark distinct glacial epochs, and suggests that they are probably parallel morainic lines of the later epoch. The loops on the coast are not so evident as in the interior; but there is a southward curve opposite Nar. Bay. The hills southward from Wickford towards Point Judith may be an intermediate moraine between Nar. Bay and Ct. River.

1882, March 11. *Providence Press.* Seekonk Coal. —

1882. C. H. HITCHCOCK. *Proc. Amer. Assoc. Adv. Science,* vol. 31, pp. 325–329. "The Glacial Flood of the Conn. River Valley."

1882. JAMES D. DANA. *Amer. Journ. Science.* "The Flood of the Connecticut River Valley from the melting of the Quaternary Glacier," vol. 23, pp. 87–97, 179–202, 360–373; vol. 24, pp. 98–104. In the last, Dana considers "The question as to the Elevation of the Land," and argues that there was a real change in *land-level* and not a mere change of *sea-level* caused by the forming of a polar ice cap of great thickness changing the center of gravity of the earth, as advocated by Adhémar, Croll, and others. Dana still adheres to his position that "the Glacial era was not for the higher latitudes generally one of *less* elevation in the land than now (as it must be by Adhémar's hypothesis), and was probably one of somewhat greater elevation for large portions."

1883. JAMES D. DANA. *Proc. Amer. Assoc. Adv. Science,* vol. 32, pp. 195–198. "Evidence from Southern New England against the Iceberg Theory of the Drift." 1. Scratches. 2. Transported bowlders. 3. Southern New Eng. not submerged more than 25 to 35 ft. Also *Science,* vol. 2. pp. 390–392.

1883. J. S. NEWBERRY. *Proc. Amer. Assoc. Adv. Science,* vol. 32. "The Ancient Glaciation of N. Amer.: its Extent, Character, and Teachings" [abstract], pp. 198–9. "The Eroding Power of Ice" [abstract]. pp. 200–1. A protest against the theories of geologists who claim that glacial ice has not played an important part in erosion. Also *Science,* vol. 2, p. 316.

1883. G. F. WRIGHT. *Proc. Amer. Assoc. Adv. Science,*

vol. 32, p. 203. Location of terminal moraine S. of New England, and parts performed by E. Hitchcock, King, C. H. Hitchcock, Upham, Cook, Smock, and others, in tracing it. Also *Science*, vol. 2, p. 316.

1883. GEO. H. STONE. *Proc. Amer. Assoc. Adv. Science*, vol. 32, pp. 234-237. "The Kame Rivers of Maine." [Abstract.] Evidence of both sub-glacial and super-glacial streams. Also *Science*, vol. 2, p. 319.

Also in vol. 32, *Amer. Assoc.*, several other papers on glacial action, mostly referring to regions west of New Eng.

1883. T. NELSON DALE. *Proc. Boston Soc. Nat. Hist.*, vol. 22, pp. 179-201. "A Contribution to the Geology of Rhode Island." This paper confines itself to the south-eastern part of the island of Aquidneck and the eastern shore of the eastern passage of Nar. Bay. Plate 1 is a geological map of that region, scale $\frac{1}{80000}$. Plate 2 is a geol. map of "Paradise" Rocks, near Newport R. I., scale $\frac{1}{10000}$. Plate 3 contains several sections.

In the first part of the paper is a list of publications relating more or less directly to the geology of the island of Rhode Island. The remaining portions of the paper state the views of previous writers and the observations of Dale upon the geology of Easton's Point (including Purgatory), Paradise and the Hanging Rocks, Wood's Castle, Taggart's Ferry, Black Point, Sandy Point, Sachuest Neck, and the Little Compton shore, with kinds of rock, dip, strike, etc.; also the author's conclusions. He alludes to *Lingulæ* shells in pebbles of quartzite conglomerate, pp. 183, 193; plant stems in boulder, p. 191; and *Annularia longifolia*, p. 193. He states two theories suggested by Prof. Wolcott Gibbs to account for the fissures in the conglomerate: 1. Wave theory. 2. Contraction theory.

1883. T. NELSON DALE. *Proceedings of The Newport Natural History Society*, Document 2.

"The Geology of the tract known as 'Paradise,' near Newport," with map and sections, pp. 3-5. This is an abstract of the paper published by the Boston Soc. Nat. Hist.

"Remarks on some of the Evidences of Geological Disturbance in the Vicinity of Newport," with plate containing 2 figures, pp. 5–8. This paper gives descriptions and localities of slickensides, plications, faults, double system of folds, fissures in the conglomerate, and dislocated veins. It also gives explanation of fissures at Purgatory and Paradise as resulting from pressure in two directions nearly at right angles, in connection with the double system of folds.

1883. EDGAR F. CLARK. *Proc. Newport Nat. Hist. Soc.*, Document 2, pp. 9–12. "Studies in the R. I. Coal Measures." He gives a list of about 60 species of coal plants found in R. I., with some discussion of the age of the *Asterophyllite* family and the character of the *Calamostachys*. He refers to the wing of an insect found at Bristol, and suggests the temporary name *Blatta Americana*. (See 1885, *Random Notes*, where another name is substituted for this.)

1883–4. JAMES D. DANA. *Amer. Journ. Science.* "On the Western discharge of the flooded Conn.; or that through Farmington Valley to New Haven," vol. 25, pp. 440–448. "Phenomena of the Glacial and Champlain Periods about the mouth of the Conn. Valley — that is, the New Haven Region." Part I. "Glacial Phenomena." Bottom of glacier flowed down the valleys in distinct streams, but when the ice was deep, the top flowed at the same time in a direction oblique to the valleys, vol. 26, pp. 341–361. Part II. "The Phenomena of the Champlain Period, or the consequences of the Glacial flood in the New Haven Region," with maps, vol 27, pp. 113–130.

Notice of Prof. Chamberlin's paper on the "Terminal Moraine of the Second Glacial Epoch." Prof. D. states that he "has not yet observed in New Eng. any facts that can be referred to a second glacial epoch"; refers to his views published in 1873 in regard to a terminal moraine deposit on Long Island from the melting southern edge of the retreating glacier, and states that "it is still true that nobody knows whether the glacier may not have extended miles outside of L. I. when at its farthest limit," the principal objection being that the terminal moraine of New Jersey is nearly in a line with the southern coast of L. I. He "has satisfied himself that the double line of elevation in L. I. was a configuration of the surface that preceded the era of glacial depositions. The underlying sands, gravels, and clays, up to a level usually of 80 ft. and often greater, are Tertiary (where not Cretaceous), and the subdivisions into high or low regions appear to have existed in these older deposits of L. I. before glacial deposition took place," vol. 28, pp. 228–231.

1884. T. NELSON DALE. *Amer. Journ. Science*, vol. 27, pp. 217–228, 282–291. " A Contribution to the Geology of Rhode Island," with geol. section and map of the south-western part of the island of Aquidneck, the southern half of Conanicut island, and the western shore of the west passage of Nar. Bay, scale $\frac{1}{80000}$. The first two pages are devoted to a re-statement of the principal points of the author's former paper. " The two papers, together, thus describe a belt across the lands which border and divide the mouth of Nar. Bay, and afford an entire section across the southern extremity of the New England Carboniferous Basin."

States the conflicting views of Jackson, E. Hitchcock, C. H. Hitchcock, Shaler, Hunt, and Crosby respecting the rocks of Newport Neck, pp. 219, 289, 290. Gives kinds of rock, dip, strike, etc., for Easton's Beach, Cliffs, Newport City, Miantonomah Hill, Coddington Cove, Bishop Rock, Coaster's Harbor Island and Rock, Gull Rocks, Goat Island, Little Lime Rock, Lime Rocks, Newport Neck, Rose Island, Conanicut, Dutch Island, Packard's Rocks, Bonnet Point, and Narragansett Pier, with stratigraphical and physiographical conclusions. On Newport shore near Narragansett Avenue is the converse of the Purgatory chasm, " the rock between two E.–W. fissures being left, while that on either side has been eroded." In Carboniferous times " the ancient shore, on the east, followed the line now indicated by the range of granite hills trending south from Tiverton towards West Island, and, on the west, that indicated by the corresponding range of Barber's Height and Tower Hill, fifteen miles distant in North and South Kingstown, which trends southward toward Point Judith." An island about 4 miles in diameter covered what is now part of Conanicut, Newport Neck, and harbor. The plowing out of the east, west, and central passages of Nar. Bay and other valleys attributed "in part to pre-glacial, but largely to glacial erosion."

1884–5. T. NELSON DALE. *Proc. Newport Nat. Hist. Soc.*, Document 3.

"The Geology of the Mouth of Narragansett Bay," pp. 5–14. This paper gives in a general and popular form, without scientific details, the results reached in the two papers published by the same author in Proc. Boston Soc. Nat. Hist. and Amer. Journ. Science. It furnishes a colored geological map of the Mouth of Nar. Bay, scale $\frac{1}{80000}$; a geological section $15\frac{1}{2}$ miles long, extending from West Island N. W. across Newport, Conanicut, and Dutch Islands to the mainland on the W. shore; and a fine artotype view of The Hanging Rock, or Berkeley's Seat, at Paradise.

Dale recognizes 9 kinds of rock in that vicinity: 1. Protogine clearly stratified (a granite with chlorite in place of mica) and gneiss; found in E. part of Newport Neck, S. part of northern extension of Conanicut, E. and W. Islands, near Nar. Pier, etc.; 1,200 ft. or more thick. 2. Mica Schist, with veins of granite; on main land N. of Nar. Pier; 1,450 ft. 3. Chlorite and Hornblende Schists; in small patches; 400 to 900 ft. 4. Chloritic Argillyte; W. part of Newport Neck, several small islands, and Little Compton; 500 to 2,000 ft. 5. Siliceous Argillyte or "flinty slate"; middle part of Newport Neck, a small part of Conanicut and Sachuest Neck; 500 to 2,000 ft. 6. Metamorphic Grit, with *Annularia longifolia;* in small patches; 750 ft. 7. Sideritic Argillyte, gray argillaceous schists; Easton's Point, most of the southern part of Conanicut, including the whole Beaver Tail and Ferry regions; 600 to 2,000 ft. 8. Quartzyte Conglomerate, with *Lingulae*; most of Easton's Point and Paradise, Purgatory, E. shore of Aquidneck Island, etc.; 750 ft. 9. Coal Measures, slates, mica schist, and fine conglomerates, with coal seams; much of the island of Aquidneck, Dutch Island, parts of Conanicut, etc.; 2,000 ft. Total 8,000 to 13,000 ft. Dale finds no igneous or eruptive rocks. Nos. 1 & 2 are the oldest, perhaps Archean; Nos. 3, 4, & 5 possibly Silurian; and Nos. 6, 7, 8, & 9 certainly Carboniferous. There is the greatest variety of rocks about Newport Neck and the southern portion of the northern part of Conanicut, near the Dumplings, there being no less than five different kinds in each of those localities. Some of the boulders in No. 8 are very large, measuring from 4 to 9 ft. in diameter. Four theories (glacier, iceberg, sea-waves, and river-current) are given to account for the formation of this conglomerate. There are no strata here of the identical character of the pebbles and boulders contained in it. The pressure of the strata in two directions and glacial action are discussed, as in other papers. The map differs from Jackson's most in the rocks of Newport Neck and the southern part of Conanicut.

" On Metamorphism in the R. I. Coal Basin," pp. 85, 86. R. I. Carboniferous rocks differ from others of the same age in being more metamorphosed. " Instead of bituminous coal or of anthracite, we find there a plumbaginous anthracite; instead of the accompanying clays and clay-slates, we find clay-slates and mica-schists." But the metamorphism of the coal measures has proceeded further than it is generally supposed to have done, even in that region. Along the West Passage of Nar. Bay, the strata of the coal-measures are more disturbed and metamorphosed than in other portions of that section of the basin. On the W. shore of the northern portion of Conanicut, Dale found mica schist and plumbaginous argillyte with garnets, staurolite, ottrelite, chlorite, quartzyte, and radiate asbestus. "If such highly crystalline Paleozoic rocks occur in one region they may occur elsewhere; and it would not be surprising if some metamorphic rocks, now regarded as of Azoic or Eozoic age, should be ultimately found to belong to the Paleozoic." Reprinted by The Newport Nat. Hist. Soc. from *Proc. Canadian Institute*, Toronto, March, 1885.

1884. J. D. WHITNEY and M. E. WADSWORTH. *Bulletin Museum Comparative Zoölogy* at Harvard College, in Cambridge, vol. 7, No. 11, pp. 331–562. "The Azoic System and its proposed subdivisions." Exhaustive discussion of the Azoic or Archean, with history, and views of prominent geologists at different times. Graphite, limestone, iron, sulphur, apatite, and *Eozoan Canadense* no evidence of life below the

Primordial; argues for term Azoic for all these older formations. Makes a distinction between graphite of older rocks and plumbago of later. Opposes the principles adopted by Logan and Hunt. Present arrangement of Canadian Survey: Laurentian, Norian, Arvonian, Huronian, Montalban, and Taconian. If the principles of that survey were to be carried out, there should be 12 divisions instead of 6, and they should be wholly lithological.

1884. J. and J. B. MARCOU. *Bulletin of the U. S. Geolog. Survey*, No. 7. " A Catalogue of Geological Maps of America, 1752–1881." Bound in vol. 2 of the Bulletins, 1885.

1884. *Random Notes on Natural History*, Providence, vol. 1. Hornblende penetrating Quartz, Calumet Hill, Cumberland, No. 1, p. 3. Magnetic Sand of Block Island, No. 2, p. 5. Rhode Island Iron, No. 5, p. 3. Quartz Crystals of Cumberland and Smithfield, No. 6, p. 6.

1884. E. B. EDDY. *Random Notes*, vol. 1, No. 4, pp. 11, 12. Porphyritic Iron Ore of Cumberland.

1884. G. F. WRIGHT. *Amer. Naturalist*, vol. 18, pp. 755–767. " The Glaciated Area of North America." With map, fig. 1, p. 756, showing terminal moraine through Block Island, Long Island, etc. Kames in New England.

1884. LEO LESQUEREUX. *Amer. Naturalist*, vol. 18, pp. 921–923. " The Carboniferous Flora of R. I." List of species, named, and description of two new species.

1884. " W." in *The R. I. Citizen*, Jan. 11. " Round Rocks" in Johnston, R. I.

1884. *Providence Journal*, May 14. " Field-Day of the Franklin Society. The 'Round Rocks' interviewed." Including poem by Geo S. Burleigh.

1884. *Providence Journal*, May 22. " Meeting of the Prov. Franklin Society," including a report of the Committee on the Geol. of R. I.

1884. *Providence Journal*, Sept. 17. " Block Island. The Strata Found in Digging Wells." Some of the wells were bored from 70 to 100 ft. deep, running far below the level of the sea, without finding a good supply of water. The strata found are composed of sand, clay, pebbles, cobble stones, and peat; but no ledge. A remarkably white, fine sand is mentioned in two instances.

1884. W. M. DAVIS. *Amer. Journ. Science*, vol. 28, pp. 407–416. "The Distribution and Origin of Drumlins." The term means a long, rounded hill. "Drumlins are hills composed of compact, unstratified glacial drift or till; their form is usually elongate or oval, with a ratio of horizontal axes varying from 6 : 1 to 1 : 1 ; the longer axis is parallel to former local glacial motion, as shown by neighboring striation or transportation of bowlders; the profile is generally smoothly arched and commonly almost symmetrical; terminal slopes, 3° to 10°; lateral slopes, 10° to 20°; length, one-eighth to two or more miles; height, 20 to 250 feet above base." The "parallel ridges," "drums and sow-backs," "lenticular hills," "whalebacks," "parallel drift-hills," and "mamillary or elliptical hills" of other authors are nearly synonymous terms. Various theories of origin stated. Davis favors the theory that they were made under glaciers in a way "similar to that by which a stream of water often makes longitudinal ridges of sand in its bed;" and thinks they "have suffered very little from post-glacial erosion." "Kames were formed close by the front of the melting and retreating ice," sometimes on the flanks of drumlins.

1884. ARTHUR B. EMMONS. *Transactions Amer. Institute Mining Engineers*. "Notes on the R. I. and Mass. Coals," 8 pp. Exploring for coal with a diamond drill. Analyses by F. A. Gooch and B. T. Putnam of nine samples of Portsmouth coal, averaging about 73 per cent. carbon; one of Cranston coal, 82 carbon, and others. "The Portsmouth coal possesses the striking peculiarity of quickly taking up a large percentage of water under a moist condition of the atmosphere, and as readily parting with it under a drier condition of the atmosphere." The percentage of water may vary 10 to 15 per cent. Fraudulent coal-core cut in Seekonk, Mass., in 1875.

1884. C. H. HITCHCOCK. Geological Map of the U. S. in
" The National Atlas," Gray, Phila. Differs from the maps
of 1874 and 1878. Silurian runs from Boston through nearly
the whole western part of the northern boundary of R. I., as
far S. as Providence, leaving the N. E. part of R. I. Carboniferous.

1884. W. J. McGEE. Geological Map of the U. S., in
" Fifth Annual Report of the U. S. Geological Survey," by J.
W. Powell, Director. R. I. Archean and Carboniferous.

1884. H. F. WALLING. " Coöperation between National
and State Governments in Topographical Surveys." Read before the Amer. Society of Civil Engineers at the Buffalo meeting, pp. 331–342.

1884–86. Reports of the Commissioners of the Topographical Survey of Mass., Francis A. Walker, Henry L. Whiting,
and N. S. Shaler.

1885. *Providence Journal*, Feb. 14, quoted from *Iron Trade Review*. " Making Iron at Tide-water." Amount and
value of Cumberland iron, and advantages of locating furnaces
on tide-water where ores, coal, limestone, and markets are
found together.

1885. JOHN W. POWELL, Director of the U. S. Geological
Survey. " On the Organization of Scientific Work of the General Government," 468 pp. Washington Government Printing
Office. Extracts from testimony taken by a Joint Commission
of Senate and House.

1885. DAVID W. HOYT. *Random Notes on Nat. Hist.*,
vol. 2, pp. 36, 37. " Soundings in and around Narragansett
Bay." Report of lecture before Franklin Society, showing the
effect if the land were raised 50 or 100 ft.

1885. *Random Notes on Nat. Hist.*, vol. 2, p. 64.
"*Mylacris Packardii*," a fossil insect found at Bristol, R. I.,
by E. F. Clark, named by Scudder. (See 1883.)

1885. MESSAGE OF GOV. BOURN to the R. I. General
Assembly. Commends the plan for an exact topographical

survey of the State by the U. S. Geological Survey and the State of R. I., jointly.

Estimated cost of the survey, $12,000, half to be paid by R. I. and half by U. S.; $3,000 per year each, for 2 years. Articles in favor, and resolutions of the Prov. Franklin Society, *Prov. Journal*, Feb. 4, 5, 7, & 10. A hearing was granted the Society the next year, reported in *Prov. Journ.*, April 1, 1886.

1886. *Providence Journal*, March 10. "Block Island Trees." Finding pine cones in a peat bed, considered by the inhabitants as evidence that the island was once wooded with pine trees.

1886. A. W. BROWN. *Providence Journal*, March 17. "Block Island. Its Trees." Hickory nuts as well as pine cones found in peat; also leaves, roots, stumps, and large logs. Distinct lignitic coal found. One peat bed 20 ft. thick, under Sandy Hill. Probably the trees grew on the main land, and these vegetable remains were transported to the island by ice or flood.

1886. *Providence Journal*, May 18. "The Wolf Rocks at Kingston."

1886. A. S. PACKARD. *Providence Journal*, May 27. "A Visit to the Wolf Rocks." Enormous boulders deposited by glacial action in a deep ravine, of pre-glacial origin, which runs N. W. and S. E. Copied in *Random Notes*, July, 1886.

1886. THOMAS J. BATTEY. *Random Notes on Nat. Hist.*, vol. 3. "Kames in R. I.," p. 81. "The Amethyst Locality of Burrillville, R. I.," pp. 90, 91.

1886. C. H. HITCHCOCK. "Geological Map of the U. S. and part of Canada," compiled "for the American Institute of Mining Engineers, to illustrate the schemes of Coloration and Nomenclature recommended by the International Geological Congress." Explained in *Transactions Amer. Inst. Min. Eng.* The Archean Era is divided into two periods only, Laurentian and Huronian. R. I. is given as Laurentian and Carboniferous, without the Silurian which appears in the map of 1884 by the same author.

1886. W. O. CROSBY and G. H. BARTON. *Proc. Boston Soc. Nat. Hist.*, vol. 23. "On the Great Dikes at Paradise, near Newport." The "amphibolic aggregate" of Pres. Hitchcock and "hornblende schist" of Dale found to be eruptive, not stratified. This reverses their previous generalization that the Carboniferous strata of N. Eng. are not traversed by eruptive rock.

1886. *Prov. Journal.* "Local Artesian Wells," Dec. 10.

"A New R. I. Industry," Dec. 30. Advocates "erecting a modern blast furnace at some point on Nar. Bay," using Cumberland iron ore and Portsmouth coal. Refers to results of experiments by W. H. Adams with Portsm. coal, given in *Engineer and Mining Journal* of Dec. 4.

1886. *Science*, vol. 8, pp. 622–3. Topographical Survey of Mass., executed jointly by U. S. Geological Survey and State of Mass. First map published, Greylock-Williamstown-North Adams district, scale 1 inch to a mile ($\frac{1}{62500}$), "with brown contours every 20 ft., blue water courses, and black roads, towns, and lettering." Value of good topographical maps, and need of "local examination of minute topographic details."

1886. T. Sterry Hunt. "Mineral Physiology and Physiography." Boston. Gives 7 different theories of the origin of crystalline or Archean rocks, including a new one proposed by Hunt, the "crenitic" theory.

1877. *Providence Journal.* "The Cove Basin. Soundings taken to determine the underlying strata," Jan. 10. Kind and thickness of strata passed through in sinking several wells in and near the Cove.

"Possibilities of Portsmouth Coal," Jan. 19. Hope of finding natural gas in Portsm. From *Fall River News.*

"Rhode Island Coal," Feb. 6. Interview with the former superintendent of the Portsm. mines, history of the work there.

1887. Message of Gov. Wetmore to the R. I. General Assembly. Calls attention to the value and importance of a geological and scientific survey of the State, and gives a history of the matter from 1875 to date.

Note.—References to other publications, received too late for insertion in the proper order, will be given in a later portion of this report.

II. CATALOGUE OF ROCKS, MINERALS, AND SOILS,
Collected during the Geological Survey of Rhode Island,
Summer of 1839.

BY CHARLES T. JACKSON, M. D.

Class 1.   Unstratified Rocks.

(Granite, Sienite, Hornblende Rock, Trap, Serpentine, Soapstone, etc.)

Granite, with Flesh-colored Feldspar, Mount Hope.
Granite, near Brande's Iron works, Richmond.
Granite, near Phillips hotel, Scituate.
Granite, coarse, Warren's Point, Little Compton.
Granite, with Black Mica, Louisquisset Turnpike, Smithfield.
Granite, west side of Harris Lime Rock, Smithfield.
Granite, Rockland factories, Scituate.
Granite, Boston Neck Point.*
Granite, vein, Boston Neck.*
Granite, Point Judith, east shore, South Kingstown.
Granite, Job Grant, Cumberland.
Granite, coarse, with White Feldspar, Boston Neck Point.
Granite, coarse, Mr. Almy's, Little Compton.
Granite, Protogine, Cumberland Hill.
Granite, coarse, Whipple Cook's, Cumberland.
Granite, Austin's Point, South Kingstown.
Granite, vein, Cumberland.
Granite, Porphyritic, Mr. Razy's, Cumberland.
Granite, Mr. Razy's, Cumberland.

---

* "Warwick" is added to these lines in manuscript No. 2, but is not found in manuscript No. 1. Probably the addition was the result of confounding Boston Neck, in South Kingstown, with Warwick Neck.

NOTE. We are not aware that this Catalogue has ever before been printed. Dr. Jackson, in his Report, says, "manuscript copies will be furnished with the three suits of specimens." Two copies of this catalogue are now in the possession of the Providence Franklin Society. One of these, which we shall call manuscript No. 1, bears upon the cover the following: "The property of C. T. Jackson, Boston." Upon one of the leaves is inscribed: "Presented to the Providence Franklin Society, by L. Holbrook, New York. Providence, August 21, 1879." It appears to be the original copy prepared by Dr. Jackson, in which specimens are not classified. Manuscript No. 2 appears to be the copy originally given to the Franklin Society with one of the three sets of specimens. It is evidently copied

Sienite, Beacon Pole Hill, Cumberland.
Sienite, Governor Knight's, Cranston.
Hornblende Rock, Clayville.
Hornblende Rock, North Providence.
Hornblende Rock, W. of Jointer ledge, Harris rock, Smithfield.
Hornblende Rock, crystalline, Cumberland Hill.
Hornblende Rock, Neutaconkanut Hill.
Hornblende Rock, Cumberland Hill.
Hornblende Rock, a variety, Smithfield.*
Hornblende Rock, William Whipple, Cumberland.*
Hornblende Rock, Hunting Hill, Cumberland.
Hornblende Rock, Iron mine, Cranston.
Greenstone Trap, dyke, North Providence.
Greenstone Trap, dyke, Middle rock, H. quarry, Smithfield.
Trap Rock with limestone, near W. Whipple's, Cumberland.
Talcose Rock, or Soapstone, William Jenkins, Cranston.
Talcose Rock, a wall in Cumberland.
Talcose Rock, Smithfield.
Talcose Rock, containing Green Talc, Smithfield.
Talcose Rock, William Whipple, Cumberland.
Talcose Rock, Brown's, Johnston.†
Serpentine Rock, (decomposed) Diamond Hill, Cumberland.
Serpentine, William Whipple, Cumberland.
Serpentine, Knight's hotel, Johnston.
Serpentine, 4 varieties, opposite the Lime Is., Newport.
Serpentine, Willow Grove, Newport.
Serpentine, light yellow, smoothed. Aaron White, Cumberland.
Epidote Rock, Tower Hill, Cumberland.
Epidote Rock, Neutaconkanut Hill.
Quartz Rock, Mansville.
Feldspar Rock, compact, Newport Neck.
Gneiss, Porphyritic Granite, North Providence.

---

from No. 1, but the specimens are arranged in a different order, rocks of the same kind being put together. The catalogue here printed is copied from manuscript No. 2, but corrected by comparison with No. 1.

Repetitions are not reprinted here, where the language in the manuscript is precisely the same, and may possibly refer to the same specimen.

* Corrected from manuscript No. 1.

† In manuscript No. 1, only.

Class 2. Stratified Primary Rocks, or Rocks of Metamorphic Origin.

(Gneiss, Mica Slate, Talcose Slate, Limestones, Altered Slates, etc.)

Gneiss, Nipmuck quarries, Scituate.
Gneiss, Cumberland Iron Hill.
Gneiss, C. Edwards.
Gneiss, Porphyritic, West Greenwich.
Gneiss, Granite, Richmond factories.
Gneiss, Smithfield.
Gneiss, Burrillville.
Gneiss, Porphyritic, Louisquisset Turnpike, North Providence.
Gneiss, Louisquisset Turnpike, Smithfield.
Gneiss, Cumberland Hill.
Gneiss, Mr. Aldrich, Smithfield.
Gneiss, Porphyritic Granite, South Kingstown Hill.
Gneiss, Granite, Rockland factories, Scituate.
Mica Slate, Z. Southgate, Smithfield.
Mica Slate, Black, North Providence.
Mica Slate, Whipple Cook's, Cumberland.
Mica Slate, C. Edwards.
Mica Slate, Black, Brande's Iron Works, Richmond.
Mica Slate, Neutaconkanut Hill.
Mica Slate, Devil's Foot ledge, North Kingstown.
Mica Slate, White, with Black Mica.
Mica Slate, South Kingstown Ferry.
Mica Slate, Blue, Woonsocket Falls.
Mica Slate, North Kingstown.
Mica Slate, scythe-stones, 6 specimens, Woonsocket.
Mica Slate, Captain Jenckes, Smithfield.
Mica Slate, Natic factories, Warwick.
Mica Slate, wall of Serpentine bed, Cumberland.
Mica Slate, Mr. Ballou, Cumberland.
Mica Slate, calciferous, loose, Cumberland.
Mica Slate, Whipple Razy's, Cumberland.
Mica Slate, passing into Grauwacke, Wickford.
Talco-micaceous Slate, green, Z. Southgate, Smithfield.
Talco-micaceous Slate, wrinkled, Z. Southgate, Smithfield.

Talco-micaceous Slate, Mansville.
Talcose Slate, or firestone, Woonsocket Hill.
Talcose Slate, Johnston.
Talcose Slate, with Tottenite, Conanicut Island.*
Talcose Slate, mostly Granular Quartz.
Chlorite Slate, W. Jenkins, Cranston.
Chlorite Slate, North Providence.
Chlorite Slate, W. Whipple's, Cumberland.
Indurated Slate, Rock farm, Newport.
Indurated Slate, Price's Neck, Newport.
Indurated Slate, Newport Neck.
Flinty Slate, Willow Grove, Newport.
Hornblende Slate, Cumberland Hill.
Slate, Newport Neck.
Slate, green, compact, Newport Neck.
Slate, from Jenkins & Man's, Smithfield.
Scoria of Slate, at junction with Grauwacke, Newport Neck, contains glazed Epidote.
Limestone, nodules in Grauwacke Slate, Newport.
Carbonate of lime, first quality, Dexter rock, Smithfield.
Carbonate of lime, blue, reticulated with white, Dext. Smithf.
Carbonate of lime, first quality, soft, Harris lime rock, Smithf.
Hard Jointer, first quality, Harris rock, Smithfield.
Magnesian Limestone, hard, Middle rock, Smithfield.
Blue Jointer, first quality, Smithfield.
Hard Jointer, first quality, Smithfield.
Calcareous Spar, Harris rock, Smithfield.
Limestone, E. Angel, Smithfield.
Translucent Limestone, Harris quarry, Smithfield.

---

*This line occurs in both manuscripts. In manuscript No. 1 it is immediately preceded by "Talcose Slate containing brown mineral, Conanicut," which does not appear in No. 2. Perhaps "Tottenite" was so named by Dr. Jackson in honor of Col. J. G. Totten, U. S. army, who had charge of the construction of Fort Adams, Newport, 1825-38, and conducted a series of experiments on the expansion and contraction of building stone by natural changes of temperature. We have not seen "Tottenite" mentioned elsewhere. Had Dr. Jackson decided it to be a distinct species, he would have published the fact. An examination of the two specimens, preserved in the cabinet of the Franklin Society, leads us to conclude that they are the "Sideritic Argillyte" of Dale, containing minute nodules of siderite, weathered to limonite on exposure. Dale remarks that these nodules. "when oxidized, give the surface of the rock a striking appearance."

Limestone, Louisquisset Turnpike, A. Arnold, Smithfield.
Limestone with Dendrites, Harris quarry, Smithfield.
Rhomboid of Rhomb Spar, Harris rock, Smithfield.
Rhomboid of Rhomb Spar, containing Silvery Talc and delicate
    Dendrites, Harris rock, Smithfield.
Argentine Limestone, Middle rock, Smithfield.
Talcose Limestone, J. Arnold, Smithfield.
Limestone, J. Arnold, Smithfield.
Green Limestone, F. Brown, Cumberland.
Limestone, granular, Cumberland.
Limestone in Chlorite Slate, W. Jenkins, Cranston.
Limestone, fine granular, Brown's quarry, Johnston.
Nail-head Calcareous Spar, with Silvery Talc, Smithfield.
Blue Limestone, North Providence.
Limestone, Mr. Whipple's, Smithfield.
Compact Limestone, Lime Island, Newport Harbor.
Limestone Breccia, shore near Fort Adams, Newport.
Limestone, buff-colored, near Fort Adams, Newport.*
Limestone, Cumberland Hill.
Magnesian Limestone, Hard Middle rock, Smithfield.
Limestone, Mr. Mason, North Providence.
Limestone, North Providence.
Yellow Limestone, North Providence.

Class 3. *Transition Grauwackes and Slates of the Coal
Formation, Coal, Plumbago, etc.*

Grauwacke, fine, compact, Peter Church's quarry, Warren.
Grauwacke, metamorphic, Swanzey, 1 mile W. Gray's P. O.
Grauwacke, metamorphic, Louisquisset Turnpike, N. Prov.
Grauwacke, junction of granite and limestone, N. Brown,
    North Providence.†
Grauwacke, junction with granite, Cranston.
Grauwacke, Cumberland coal mines.

---

*At this point in the manuscripts are inserted the analyses of 13 specimens of Rhode Island limestones. With one exception, these are apparently included in the more complete table of 18 specimens printed on p. 246 of Jackson's Report; but the order of arrangement, the language, and in some cases the figures, are different. No. 3 in the printed table should have 40.6 instead of 46.6 insoluble matter; and there are various other differences.

† Johnston in manuscript No. 1.

Grauwacke, Pawtucket.
Grauwacke, Seekonk, one mile from Providence.
Grauwacke, passing into mica slate, North Kingstown.
Grauwacke, suitable for the quarry, Pappoose-squaw's Neck, Bristol.
Grauwacke, fine, Miantonomah Hill, Newport.
Grauwacke, Louisquisset Turnpike, North Providence.
Grauwacke, North Providence.
Grauwacke, fine, Wrentham.
Grauwacke, fine red, Mansfield.
Grauwacke, red, Attleboro.
Grauwacke, indurated, W. Razy's, Cumberland.
Grauwacke Slate, indurated, Rumstick Point, Warren.
Grauwacke Slate, near Cranston Bank.
Grauwacke Slate, metamorphic, North Kingstown.
Grauwacke Slate, metamorphic, North Providence.
Grauwacke Slate, green, Swanzey.
Grauwacke Slate, Swanzey.
Grauwacke Slate, Louisquisset Turnpike, North Providence.
Grauwacke Slate, Cumberland.
Grauwacke Slate, Ezra Blake's, Cumberland.
Grauwacke Slate, Hunting Hill, Cumberland.
Grauwacke Slate, Fort Adams, Newport.
Grauwacke Slate, altered, Hunting Hill, Cumberland.
Grauwacke Slate, containing Yellow Ochre, shore near Fort Adams, Newport.
Grauwacke Slate, metamorphic, Slate Hill, Johnston.
Coarse Conglomerate, loose, Bristol.
Coarse Conglomerate. loose, Pappoose-squaw's Neck, Bristol.
Coarse Conglomerate, quartz pebbles, Purgatory, Newport.
Coarse Conglomerate, containing numerous small crystals of Magnetic Iron ore, Purgatory, Newport.
Coarse Conglomerate, top of Miantonomah Hill, Newport.
Coarse Conglomerate, Attleboro.*
Anthracite, Case's mine, Portsmouth, 3 per cent. ashes.
Anthracite, Kilkenny, Ireland, 5 per cent. ashes.

---

* In manuscript No. 1, only.

Anthracite, Portsmouth refuse, 22 and 24 per cent. ashes.
Anthracite, Cumberland coal selected by Mr. Mason, 15.4 per cent. ashes.
Anthracite, Cumberland coal from agent of the mine, 31 per cent. ashes.
Anthracite, well near Providence, 28 per cent. ashes.
Anthracite, second bed, Harden's, Mansfield.
Anthracite, first bed, Harden's, Mansfield.
Anthracite, Skinner's vein, Mansfield.
Anthracite, containing Asbestus, Sockanosset Hill, Cranston.
Anthracite, Sockanosset Hill, Cranston.
Anthracite, Portsmouth.
Anthracite, Newport.
Plumbago, Tower Hill, Cumberland.
Impressions of Ferns, in Carbonaceous Slate, Sockanosset Hill, Cranston.
Impressions of Ferns, Portsmouth.
Impressions of Ferns, Newport Neck.
Impressions of Ferns, P. Church, Bristol Neck.
Impressions of Ferns, Durfee's ledge, Cranston.
Impressions of Ferns, Warwick Neck.
Impressions of Ferns, Wrentham.
Substitution of Calamites by Pyrites, Cranston.
Calamite, Newport Neck.
Calamite, Portsmouth mine.

Class 4. Tertiary Clays and Sands.

[Not filled out.]

Class 5. Diluvium, etc.

Cumberland Iron Boulders from Pappoose-squaw's Neck.

Class 6. Alluvium and Soils.

[See Tables, Soils of Rhode Island, printed in Jackson's Report, pp. 241–244.]

[Also Peats, p. 245.]

List of Simple Minerals.

Sulphuret of Molybdena, Cumberland.
Sulphuret of Molybdena, Cumberland Hill.
Argentiferous Galena and Blende, veins in talcose slate, or firestone, Uxbridge.
Copper Pyrites, old copper mine, Cumberland, two large and rich specimens in magnetic iron ore.
Copper Pyrites in hornblende rock, Cumberland.
Copper Pyrites, old copper mine, Cumberland.
Copper Pyrites in quartz, Middle rock, Smithfield.
Copper Pyrites in granular limestone, F. Brown, Cumberland.
Carbonate of Copper on Iron ore, Cumberland.
Carbonate of Copper, Copper Pyrites, and Hornblende, Cumberland.
Iron Pyrites, coal mines, Cumberland.
Iron Pyrites, crystallized, in a nodule of argillaceous iron ore, Newport Neck.
Iron Pyrites in slate, Newport Neck.
Hematite, stalactital, Cumberland.
Hematite, compact, Cumberland.
Hematite, botryoidal, Cumberland.
Hematite, loose, Rock farm, Newport.
Botryoidal Red Hematite, Aaron White, Cumberland.
Brown Hematite, old iron mine, Cranston.
Bog Iron ore, Bennett's, Foster.
Bog Iron ore, Harris, Cranston.
Bog Iron ore, Foster Banking Co.
Bog Iron ore, Potter's, Providence.
Bog Iron ore, Block Island.
Yellow Ochre, Cumberland.

NOTE. It will be seen that the distinction between rocks and minerals is not sharply drawn in this catalogue. Each specimen is printed in the class in which Dr. Jackson placed it. Simple minerals of the same species are printed together in these pages, however, for convenience of reference. In both of the manuscripts they are not arranged by either species or localities. The order of arrangement of the simple minerals in the manuscripts may possibly be that of collecting or receiving the specimens.

Magnetic Iron, octahedral crystals in slate, Johnston.
Magnetic Iron ore, granular, Cumberland Hill.
Magnetic Iron ore, granular, Cumberland.
Magnetic Iron ore, granular, containing Copper Pyrites, Cumberland Hill.*
Magnetic Iron ore, granular, Mansville (loose.)
Iron ore, granular, Cumberland.
Iron ore, with Asbestus, W. Whipple, Cumberland.
Iron ore, containing Carbonate of Lime, Block Island.
Iron stone, Block Island.
Titaniferous Magnetic Iron ore, porphyritic, Cumberland.
Titaniferous Magnetic Iron ore, containing Serpentine, iron mine, Cumberland.
Titaniferous Iron ore, Cumberland.
Native Copperas, Newport Neck.
Copperas Marl, Newport Neck.
Black oxide of Manganese, iron mine, Cumberland.
Fluor Spar, near Diamond Hill, Cumberland.
Gypsum crystals in iron ore, from pyrites, Newport Neck.
Brown Spar in talcose rock, Neutaconkannt Hill.
Brown Spar in talcose rock, Smithfield.
Milk Quartz, Mount Hope, Bristol.
Milk Quartz, from a vein, Smithfield.
Crystallized Quartz, Cumberland.
Smoky Quartz crystal, Aaron White.
Quartz Rock, Diamond Hill, Cumberland.
Granular Quartz, Woonsocket Hill.
Quartz crystals in Agate, Diamond Hill, Cumberland.
Druses of Quartz crystals in Agate, Diam. Hill, Cumberland.
Druses of Quartz crystals on Agate, Cumberland.
Large mass of Agate cavities filled with crys. of Quartz, Cumb.
Agate, Diamond Hill, Cumberland.
Fortification Agate, Diamond Hill, Cumberland.
Ribbon Agate, Diamond Hill, Cumberland.
Calcedony, Cumberland.
Calcedony, Diamond Hill, Cumberland.

---

* In manuscript No. 1, only.

Cacholong, Diamond Hill, Cumberland.
Prase, Cumberland.
Brown Jasper, Smithfield, loose.
Sahlite on Magnetic Iron ore, Cumberland.
Hornblende, crystallized, Cumberland.
Hornblende, R. I. mine, Cranston.*
Actinolite penetrating Quartz, Cumberland.
Ligneous Actinolite and red silicate of Manganese, Cumb.
Actinolite, vein in silicate of Manganese, Cumberland Hill.
Actinolite, Brown's, Johnston.
Actinolite, near iron mine, Cranston.
Radiated Tremolite, W. Whipple's, serpentine locality, Cumb.
Tremolite, in green limestone. F. Brown, Cumberland.
Tremolite, Smithfield.
Tremolite, Cumberland.
Asbestus, two large masses, Smithfield.
Asbestus, in carbonaceous slate, Bristol Neck.
Nephrite,† rich green, on limestone, Middle rock, Harris quarry, Smithfield.
Nephrite, large mass, yellow green, translucent, Smithfield.
Nephrite, mixed with limestone, Smithfield.
Nephrite, I. Arnold, Smithfield.
Knebelite, grey silicate of Manganese and Iron, Cumb. Hill.
Garnets in mica slate, loose, Natic factories.
Epidote, 6 varieties, Tower Hill, Cumberland.
Epidote, Newport Neck.
Epidote in Quartz, Newport Neck.
Epidote, Smithfield.
Brown Epidote, Smithfield.
Zoisite, Cumberland.
Zoisite, a beautiful specimen, Aaron White, Cumberland.
Zoisite, a crystal, Smithfield.
Black Mica, in granite, C. Edwards.*
Feldspar, flesh-colored, from a granite vein in Potter's Hill, Hopkinton.

---

* In manuscript No. 1, only.
† Since called Bowenite.

Green Talc, iron mine, Cumberland.
Green Talc, Brown's quarry, Johnston.
Light Talc, near Brown's quarry, Johnston.
Green Talc, Johnston.
Silvery Talc, Harris quarries, Smithfield.
Green Talc, Smithfield.
Soapstone rock, from wall 2 miles from Cumberland Hill.
Chlorite in protogine, Cumberland.
Chlorite. Smithfield.
Chlorite, 2 miles from Cumberland towards Smithfield.
Chlorite in limestone, North Providence.
Chlorite rock, Brown's, Johnston.
Chlorite rock, Capt. Jenkes, Smithfield.
Masonite, Natic factories, Warwick.

The set of Rhode Island rocks and minerals preserved by the Franklin Society is the only one of the three sets mentioned by Dr. Jackson which we have been able to find; neither have we been able to find any other copy of Jackson's catalogue than the two now in the possession of the Franklin Society.

III. Catalogue of Fossils Found in Rhode Island.

Carboniferous Flora of Rhode Island.

Filicaceæ. (*Ferns.*)

Sphenopteris fruciformis, Lesqx., a new species, described in the American Naturalist, vol. 18, p. 922.

Sphenopteris pseudo-Murrayana, Lesqx., described pp. 271-2, P. [*Pecopteris Murrayana*, Ill. Report of Lesqx.]

Sphenopteris Gravenhorstii,* Brgt., described pp. 274-5 and

---

* *S. Dubuissonis?* Brgt., descr. p. 275, P.; fig. by Tesch, pl. 35, b, as found in the Narragansett basin. Lesqx., in P., says the only specimen seen by him may represent *S. Gravenhorstii*; but does not give it as found in Rhode Island.

Note. This list of fossils, so far as the plants are concerned, is mainly copied from the one published by Leo Lesquereux in the American Naturalist in 1884; vol. 18, pp. 921-923. He there gives eighty-eight species, of which fifty-six are ferns. Three other species of ferns, *Dictyopteris obliqua, Alethopteris aquilina* and *A. Serlii*, though not included in the American Naturalist list, are else-

PLATE II.

Fig. 1.—*Callipteridium*, new species, or variety of *Alethopteris urophylla*, Brgt. ($\times \frac{1}{2}$.)

Fig. 2.—*Sphenopteris fruciformis*, Lesqx. ($\times \frac{1}{2}$.)

763–4, P.: figured plate ci, figures 1–1*b*, P. Also fig. by Tesch., pl. 35, fig. *g*.

Sphenopteris chærophylloides, (Brgt.) St., descr. pp. 270–1, P.

Sphenopteris cristata, St., descr. pp. 273–4 and 761–2, P.; fig. pl. cii, 1, 1*a*, and civ, 5, 5*a*, P.

Sphenopteris Salisburyi, a new species, from Mansfield, owned by Charles M. Salisbury. Examined and named by Lesquereux, in May, 1887; described by him as follows:—

"Frond tri-polypinnately divided; secondary pinnæ lanceolate; ultimate pinnæ short, linear-lanceolate, composed of alternate, oblique, small, globose or ovate indusia of fructifications in five pairs and a terminal single one, upon each pinna, joined to the rachis by short, oblique, filiform pedicels.

---

where given by Lesquereux as found in Rhode Island. (See pp. 147, xxxv, 867-8, P.) Any species not otherwise marked, therefore, is given on the authority of Lesquereux.

The species marked [E. F. C.] were published by Edgar F. Clark in the Proceedings of The Newport Natural History Society, 1883, Document 2, pp. 11, 12; but are not published in the three Rhode Island lists of Lesquereux. Two species there given are here omitted as doubtful, by Mr. Clark. Clark also gives *Dictyopteris obliqua* and many others which are included in the Lesquereux lists; but he does not give the *Alethopteris* species. We have seen the latter ascribed to Rhode Island only on page 867, P.

The species marked [C. H. H.] were published by C. H. Hitchcock in the Proceedings of the American Association for the Advancement of Science, vol. 14, 1860 [see pp. 18–20 of this report], as named by Lesquereux; but are not found in the later Rhode Island lists of Lesquereux.

The species marked ['87.] have not before been published as found in Rhode Island. The specimens to which these names are given have all been examined and labeled by Lesquereux, most of them in May, 1887.

So far as the carboniferous flora is concerned, no attempt is made to distinguish between the coal fields of Rhode Island and Massachusetts. E. Hitchcock, in the Massachusetts Report, 1841, gives drawings of *Neuropteris*, *Sphenopteris*, *Pecopteris*, *Calamites*, *Asterophyllites*, *Sphenophyllum*, *Annularia*, *Stigmaria*, etc.; but without specific names.

The references to descriptions, figures, and lists, marked P., are to the Pennsylvania Report of Lesquereux described on pages 40, 41 of this report. Those marked Tesch. are to the Boston Journal of Natural History, 1846, vol. 5, pp. 370–385.

The abbreviations for authorities are as follows:—

Brgt., Brongniart.	Ll. & Hutt., Lindley and Hutton.
Bunb'y, Bunbury.	Newb'y, Newberry.
Gein., Geinitz.	Roem., Roemer.
Germ., Germar.	Schloth., Schlotheim.
Goepp., Goeppert.	Schp., Schimper.
Gutb., Gutbier.	Scud., Scudder.
Hoffm., Hoffman.	St., Sternberg.
Lesqx., Lesquereux.	Tesch., Teschemacher.

"The species is closely related to *Sphenopteris Crepini*, Zeiller. "Fl. Foss. du bassin houiller de Valenciennes," of which work the atlas only is yet published; differing by the globose indusia smaller, more proximate, regularly alternate upon each pinnule. The pinnules are also close, at equal distance, slightly oblique, regularly alternate upon a narrow, flat rachis, which, like the involucres or indusia, is covered by short woolly filaments. The surface of the indusia is obscured by these filaments, which may be fragments of scales or involucres. The plant is also comparable to *Sphenopteris delicatula*, St., as illustrated, with its fructifications, by Kidston, Quarter. Journ. of the Geol. Soc. of London, 1884. Pl. xxv, f. 2, a fragment showing the fructifications in early stage.

"The species is very interesting, and, if published, should be carefully figured."

Sphenopteris mediana, Lesqx., descr. p. 271, P. Specific name *intermedia* used by Lesqx. in 1858, but changed to *mediana* in Report P. [C. H. H. and E. F. C.]

Sphenopteris (*Hymenophyllites*) *elegans*, Brgt., descr. pp. 287–8, P.; fig. pl. lv, 6, 6a, P.

Sphenopteris (*Hymen.*) *Hoeninghausii*, Brgt., descr. pp. 288–290, P.; fig. pl. lv, 5, 5a, P.

Sphenopteris (*Hymen.**) *tridactylites*, Brgt., descr. pp. 284–286, P.; fig. pl. lv, 8, 9b, P.

Sphenopteris or *Eremopteris* species, apparently new. Too small for a satisfactory diagnosis; like *Sphenopteris Geikii*, Kidston. E. F. Clark, from Middletown. ['87.]

Neuropteris cordata,† Brgt., descr. pp. 91–2, P.

Neuropteris hirsuta, Lesqx., descr. pp. 88–9, P.; fig. pl. viii, 1, 4, 5, 7, 9, 12, P.

Neuropteris Agassizi, Lesqx., descr. pp. 117–8, P.; fig. pl. xvii, 1–4, P. Also fig. by Tesch., pl. 34.

---

* *Hymenophyllites*, mentioned by E. F. C., is given as a subgenus of both *Rhacophyllum* and *Sphenopteris*, by Lesqx., in Report P.; but not as a separate genus.

†Jackson figures a species which he calls *N. Scheuchzeri*, Brgt. Lesquereux considers *N. Scheuchzeri* a form of *N. cordata*.

PLATE III.

FIG. 1.—*Sphenopteris Salisburyi*, Lesqx.
FIG. 2.—"*Money Stone.*" (X 1.)

FROM PHOTOGRAPHS BY R. L. P. MASON.

Neuropteris crenulata?, Brgt., descr. pp. 116-7, P.; fig. pl. xvi. 9-11*a*, P. A specimen found by D. W. Hoyt, in Providence, in 1887, was labeled by Lesqx. without the interrogation.

Neuropteris Desorii, Lesqx., descr. pp. 112-3, P.; fig. pl. xiv, 1-7 and xv, 1, P.

Neuropteris Germari, Goepp., descr. pp. 113-115, P.; fig. pl. xviii, 3-5, P.

Neuropteris heterophylla, Brgt., given under *N. angustifolia*, Brgt., by Lesqx., in P., which latter is descr. pp. 89-91 and 734, P.; fig. pl. viii, 2. 3, 6, 8, 10, 11, P. Tesch. gives both *N. angustifolia* and *N. heterophylla* as found at Mansfield.

Neuropteris tenuifolia,* Brgt., descr. pp. 100-102, P.; fig. pl. xii, 1?, 2-9, P.

Neuropteris trichomanoides, Brgt., descr. pp. 79-80, P.; fig. pl. iv, 4, P. Brown Univ., from Pawtucket. ['87.]

Neuropteris vermicularis, Lesqx., descr. pp. 99-100, P.; fig. pl. x, 5-10, P. [E. F. C.]

Neuropteris plicata, St., descr. pp. 96-7, P.; fig. pl. x, 1-4, P. [E. F. C.]

Neuropteris fimbriata, Lesqx., descr. pp. 81-2, P.; fig. pl. v, 1-6, P. [E. F. C.] Called *Cyclopteris fimbriata* by Lesqx., in 1858.

Neuropteris Clarksoni, Lesqx., descr. pp. 94-5, P.; fig. pl. ix, 1-6, P. [E. F. C.] Also found by D. W. Hoyt, in Providence, in 1887.

Neuropteris Loschii, Brgt., descr. pp. 98-9 P.; fig. pl. xi, 1-4. [C. H. H. and E. F. C.]

Cyclopteris species, put under *Neuropteris* by Lesqx., in P.

Dictyopteris Scheuchzeri, Hoffm., descr. p. 832, P.; figured by Roehl.

Dictyopteris obliqua, Bunb'y, descr. pp. 146-7, P.; fig. pl. xxiii, 4-6, P.

---

* *Neuropteris flexuosa*, Brgt., given by Tesch. and C. H. H., is put under *N. plicata* and *N. tenuifolia*, by Lesqx., in Report P., though *N. flexuosa* was used by him in 1858.

Callipteridium, new species, or variety of *Alethopteris urophylla*, Brgt., descr. Am. Naturalist, vol. 18, p. 922.

Alethopteris aquilina, Schloth.—Schp.—Lesqx., descr. pp. 181-2, P.

Alethopteris Serlii, Brgt.—Goepp., descr. pp. 176-7, P. ; fig. pl. xxix. 1-5, P. Also probably fig. by Jackson as *Pecopteris Serlii*, pl. iii, 6 ; and by Tesch., pl. 35, a,a.

Alethopteris Pennsylvanica, Lesqx., descr. p. 181, P. ; fig. Geol. Penn., 1858, pl. xi, f. 1, 2. [C. H. H.]

Odontopteris alpina, Gein., descr. pp. 126-7, P. ; fig. pl. xix. 1-5, P.

Odontopteris obtusa, Brgt. Specimen in Brown University cabinet, from Warwick. ['87.] *O. obtusa* is put under *O. alpina*, and not described as a separate species, in P.

Odontopteris alata, Lesqx., descr. pp. 131-2, P. ; fig. pl. xxi, 1, P.

Odontopteris Brardii, Brgt., descr. pp. 132-3, P. ; fig. pl. xxi, 2, P. Also descr. and fig. by Tesch., pp. 382-3, pl. 33.

Odontopteris deformata, Lesqx., descr. pp. 141-2 and 743, P. ; fig. pl. xcvii, 5, P.

Odontopteris neuropteroides, Newb'y—Roem., descr. p. 740, P. ; fig. pl. xcvii, 1-3, P.

Odontopteris patens, Lesqx., descr. pp. 740-1, P. ; fig. pl. xcvii, 7, P.

Odontopteris Schlotheimii, Brgt., descr. pp. 136-7, P. ; fig. pl. xx, 1, 2, P. [E. F. C.]

Odontopteris species, apparently new. Too small for diagnosis and determination. D. W. Hoyt, from Providence. ['87.]

Pecopteris polymorpha, Brgt., pp. 247-8. P.

Pecopteris acuta, Brgt., descr. pp. 241-2, P.

Pecopteris abbreviata?, Brgt., descr. pp. 248-9, P. ; fig. pl. xlvi, 4-6a, P.

Pecopteris cyathea, Brgt., p. 231, P. ; fig. by Tesch., pl. 36, c, and by Jackson. pl. iv, 9.

Pecopteris Miltoni, Brgt., descr. p. 247, P. ; fig. pl. xli, 9, 9a, P.

Pecopteris oreopteridis,* (Schloth.) Brgt., descr. pp. 238-9, P. ; fig. pl. xli, 8, 8a. P.

Pecopteris Cistii,* Brgt., descr. pp. 243-4, P. ; fig. xli, 4, 4a, P. [Tesch., only, at Mansfield.]

Pecopteris Bucklandi,* Brgt., descr. pp. 244-5, P.; fig. by Jackson, pl. ii, 3. [Jackson, only.]

Pecopteris Candolliana,† Brgt., descr. p. 243, P.

Pecopteris dentata, Brgt., descr. pp. 240-1, P. ; fig. pl. xliv. 4, 4a, P.

Pecopteris arborescens, (Schloth.) Brgt., descr. pp. 230-232, P. ; fig. pl. xli, 6-7b, P. Also fig. by Jackson, pl. i, 1.

Pecopteris aspidioides, Brgt., descr. p. 756, P.

Pecopteris Clarkii, Lesqx., descr. pp. 261-2, P ; fig. pl. xli, 10, 10a, P.

Pecopteris erosa, Gutb., descr. pp. 255-6, P. ; fig. pl. xliv. 1, 1a, 3, P.

Pecopteris pennæformis, Brgt., descr. pp. 239-40, P. ; fig. pl. xlv, 1-2a, P.

Pecopteris platyrachis, Brgt., descr. pp. 232-3, P. ; fig. pl. xli, 5, 5a, P.

Pecopteris quadratifolia, Lesqx., descr. pp. 234 and 756-7, P. ; fig. pl. c, 1, 2, P.

Pecopteris cristata, Gutb., descr. p. 256, P. ; fig. pl. xliv. 2, 2a, P. Specimens in Brown University cabinet, from Warwick. ['87.]

Pecopteris villosa, Brgt., descr. pp. 253-255, P. Rachis and pinna, E. F. Clark, from Bristol. ['87.]

Pecopteris (*Goniopteris*) *unita*, Brgt., descr. pp. 223-225, P. ; fig. pl. xl, 1-7b, P. Also fig. by Jackson, pl ii, 4.

---

* These three species are said by Lesqx. to be closely allied, and difficult to separate, especially in specimens from Rhode Island coal, where the nervation of small fragments of ferns is rarely distinct.

† *Pecopteris affinis*, Brgt., given by C. H. H. and E. F. C., is put under *P. Candolliana*, by Lesqx., in Report P. *P. affinis*, labeled by Lesqx., is also found in Brown University cabinet, from Warwick.

Pecopteris (Goniopteris) emarginata, Goepp., descr. pp. 225-6, P.; fig. pl. xxxix, 11. P. Specimens in Brown University cabinet, from Warwick. ['87.]

Pecopteris (Goniopteris) arguta, Brgt., descr. pp. 227-8, P.; fig. pl. xli, 2-3a, P.

Pecopteris (Goniopteris) longifolia, Brgt., descr. p. 226, P.; fig. by Tesch. pl. 36, c. [Given only by Tesch., as from Portsmouth, R. I.] Lesqx. says " very rarely found."

Pseudopecopteris* cordato-ovata,† (Weiss) Lesqx., descr. pp. 205-6, P.; fig. pl. xxxvii, 4, 5, P.

Pseudopecopteris nervosa,‡ (Brgt.) Lesqx., descr. pp. 197-8, P.; fig. pl. xxxiv, 1-3, P.

Pseudopecopteris dimorpha, Lesqx., descr. pp. 201 and 750-1, P.; fig. pl. xxxv, 1-6 and xcviii, 4. 4a, P.

Pseudopecopteris Pluckneti,§ (Brgt.) Lesqx., descr. pp. 199-201, P.; fig. pl. xxxiv, 4, 4a, and xxxv, 7, 7a, P.

Pseudopecopteris anceps, Lesqx., descr. pp. 207-8, P.; fig. pl. xxxviii, 1-4, P.

Pseudopecopteris muricata, (Brgt.) Lesqx., descr. pp. 203-205, P.; fig. pl. xxxvii, 2-2b, P. Given as *Pecopteris muricata*, Brgt., by Tesch.

Pseudopecopteris spinulosa, Lesqx., descr. pp. 195-6, P.; fig. pl. lvi, 1, 1a, P.

---

* A number of species described by Brongniart and other authors as *Pecopteris, Sphenopteris*, or *Alethopteris*, have, on account of their peculiar characters, been separated by Lesquereux, in his later works, under the name of *Pseudopecopteris*. See P., pp. 189-190.

†Lesquereux states, in P., that he was formerly disposed to consider the Wilkesbarre plant named *P. cordato-ovata*, as *Pecopteris Loschii*, Brgt. Tesch. gives *Pecopteris Loschii*, Brgt., among those found at Mansfield.

Teschemacher also gives *Pecopteris borealis*, Brgt., and *Pecopteris gigantea*, Brgt., as found at Mansfield; but Lesqx. does not mention them in P. as found in the United States.

‡*Pecopteris nervosa*, Brgt., given by C. H. H. and E. F. C.; and *Alethopteris nervosa*, given by C. H. H.; are put under *Pseudopecopteris nervosa* by Lesqx., in Report P.

§*Alethopteris Pluckneti*, Gein., given by C. H. H. and E. F. C., and *Pecopteris Pluckneti*, Brgt., are put under *Pseudopecopteris Pluckneti* by Lesqx., in Report P.

CATALOGUE OF FOSSILS.   75

Pseudopecopteris abbreviata, Lesqx., descr. p. 203. P. ; fig. Geol. Penn., 1858, pl. ix, f. 1. 1*b*. [C. H. H.] Called *Sphenopteris abbreviata* by Lesqx. in 1858, and so given by Hitch.

Pseudopecopteris irregularis, St., descr. pp. 211-212. P. ; fig. pl. lii, 1-3*b*, 8, P.   Pinnules, C. M. Salisbury, from Mansfield. ['87.]

Rhacophyllum affine, Lesqx., p. 319, P.

Rhacophyllum* Clarkii, Lesqx., descr. pp. 319-20. P. ; fig. pl. lvii, 5, P.

Rhacophyllum filiforme, (Gutb.) Lesqx., descr. p. 838, P.

Rhacophyllum filiciforme, (Gutb.) Schp., descr. pp. 316-7, P.

Rhacophyllum fimbriatum, Lesqx., descr. pp. 318-9, P.

Rhacophyllum hirsutum, var. *affine*, Lesqx., descr. p. 318, P. ; fig. pl. lvii, 2, P.

Rhacophyllum corallinum, Lesqx., descr. p. 317, P. ; fig. pl. lvii, 4, 4*a*, P.   [E. F. C.]

Rhacophyllum adnascens, Ll. & Hutt., descr. pp. 321-2. P. ; fig. pl. lvii, 9-11, P.   C. M. Salisbury, from Mansfield. ['87.]

Noeggerathia species. [E. F. C.] Lesqx. used this name for a genus in 1858, but in Report P. has substituted *Archæopteris* for it.

Rhachiopteris species.—Rachis of fern. genus descr. p. 331, P.

Calamarieæ.

Calamites Suckowii, Brgt., var. *nodosus*, St., descr. pp. 20-1, P. ; fig. pl. i, 3, 4, P.   A fine specimen.

Calamites approximatus, Schloth., descr. pp. 26-7, P. ; fig. pl. i, 5, P.   A twisted fragment.

Calamites ramosus, Brgt., descr. pp. 22-3 and 702-3, P. ; fig. pl. i, 2 and xcii, 1, 4, P.   Crushed branches.

Calamites Cistii, Brgt., descr. p. 27, P. ; fig. pl. i, 6, P.

Calamites cannæformis, Schloth., descr. pp. 24-5, P. ; fig. pl. i, 1, P.   [E. F. C.]

---
*Aphlebia, given by C. H. H., is put under *Rhacophyllum*, by Lesqx., in Report P.

Bornia radiata, (Brgt.) Schp., descr. pp. 30–1 and 706–708, P. ; fig. pl. xci, 5, and xciii, 2, P. [E. F. C.]

Asterophyllites sublævis, Lesqx., descr. p. 38, P. ; fig. Geol. Penn., 1858, pl. i, f. 3.

Asterophyllites equisetiformis, Brgt., descr. pp. 35–6, P. ; fig. pl. ii, 3, 3a, P.

Asterophyllites grandis, St., descr. p. 41, P.

Asterophyllites rigidus, Gein., descr. p. 37, P.

Asterophyllites foliosus, Ll. & Hutt., descr. pp. 38–41, P. Brown Univ. and E. F. Clark, from Bristol and Middletown. ['87.]

Asterophyllites longifolius, Brgt. ; descr. pp. 36–7, P. E. F. Clark, from Sachuest Point. ['87.]

Annularia longifolia,* Brgt., descr. pp. 45–47, P. ; fig. pl. ii, 1–2aa, and pl. iii, 10, 12, P. A large form.

Annularia calamitoides, Schp., descr. p. 48, P.

Annularia inflata, Lesqx., descr. pp. 47–8, P. ; fig. pl. ii, 2b, 2bb, P.

Annularia sphenophylloides,† Gutb., descr. pp. 48–9 and 724 ; fig. pl. ii, 8, 9, and iii, 13, P.

Sphenophyllum oblongifolium, Germ., descr. pp. 57–8, P.

Sphenophyllum Schlotheimii, Brgt., descr. pp. 52–3, P. ; fig. pl. ii, 6, 7, P.

Sphenophyllum emarginatum,‡ Brgt., descr. p. 53, P.

Sphenophyllum filiculme, Lesqx., descr. pp. 58–9, P.

Sphenophyllum longifolium, Germ., descr. pp. 53–4 and 726, P. ; fig. pl. xci, 6, P.

---

*Annularia fertilis, St., given by C. H. H., is put under *A. longifolia*, by Lesqx., in Report P.

Jackson's pl. vi, 11, named *Asterophyllites*, seems to be *Annularia*; and his pl. iii, 7, named *Equisetum*, seems to be *Asterophyllites*. The *Annularia* were probably water plants, and the *Asterophyllites* are supposed to be branches of *Calamites*.

†*Annularia brevifolia*, Brgt., given by E. F. C., is put under *A. sphenophylloides* by Lesqx., in Report P.

‡Teschemacher also gives *S. truncatum*, Brgt., and *S. dentatum*, Brgt., as found at Mansfield. The latter is given under *S. erosum*, Ll. & Hutt., by Lesqx.; descr. p. 55, P. Lesquereux states that the former is no species of Brongniart, and has not been mentioned by any author but Teschemacher.

Sphenophyllum bifurcatum, Lesqx., descr. pp. 55-6, P.; fig. pl. ii, 10, 10a. P. [E. F. C.]

Calamostachys ovalis, Lesqx., descr. pp. 717-8, P.; fig. pl. lxxxix, 3, 4; fruiting spikes of *Asterophyllites*. E. F. Clark, from Bristol. ['87.]

Calamostachys prælongus, Lesqx., descr. pp. 59-60. P. [E. F. C.] These spikes were afterwards named *Volkmannia prælonga* by Lesqx., p. 720, P.

Macrostachya lanceolata, Lesqx., descr. pp. 721-2. P. C. H. Hitchcock gives *Asterophyllites lanceolata* as occurring at Wrentham, Mass. Lesqx. described a spike in 1858 as *A. lanceolatus*, which is put under *A. foliosus*, p. 38, P.; but afterwards under *M. lanceolata*, as above. Lesqx. does not give these spikes in his R. I. list; but Hitchcock's specimen was named by him in 1860.

Lycopodinceæ.

Lepidodendron longifolium. Brgt., descr. pp. 373-4, P. Tuft of leaves.

Lepidodendron dichotomum, St.—Leaves descr. pp. 384-5.

Lepidodendron (Bergeria) quadratum, St., descr. pp. 382-3, P.; fig. pl. lxiv, 18, P.?

Lepidodendron aculeatum, St., descr. pp. 371-2, P.; fig. pl. lxiv. 1, P.

Lepidophyllum* lanceolatum, Brgt., and *Lepidostrobus lanceolatus*, descr. pp. 436-7, P.; fig. pl. lxix, 38, P.

Lepidophyllum fallax, Lesqx., descr. p. 786, P.; fig. pl. cvii, 4, 5. P.

Lepidophyllum hastatum, Lesqx., and *Lepidostrobus hastatus*, Lesqx., descr. pp. 438-9, P.; fig. pl. lxix, 27, 28, P.

Lepidophyllum majus, Brgt.—Lesqx., descr. p. 449, P.

Lepidophyllum oblongifolium, Lesqx., and *Lepidostrobus oblongifolius*, Lesqx., descr. pp. 437-8, P.; fig. pl. lxix, 29, P.

---

* *Lepidophyllum* species represent blades or bracts of *Lepidostrobus*.

Lepidophyllum Stantoni, Lesqx.

Lepidophyllum tumidum, Lesqx., descr. pp. 448 and 788, P.; fig. pl. cvii, 12, P.

Sigillaria reniformis, Brgt., descr. pp. 501-2, P.; fig. pl. lxx, 5-9, P. [E. F. C.]

Sigillaria lævigata, Brgt., descr. pp. 500-1, P.; fig. pl. lxxi, 1-3, P. E. F. Clark, from Newport. ['87.]

Sigillaria mammillaris, Brgt., descr. pp. 483-485 and 799, P.; fig. pl. lxxii, 5, 6 and cviii, 6, P. E. F. Clark, from Middletown. ['87.]

Stigmaria ficoides, Brgt.—Goepp., descr. pp. 514-516, P.; fig. pl. lxxiv, 1-4, P. Leaves obliquely crossing clay, and specimens of other leaves.

Spirangium multiplicatum, Lesqx., descr. pp. 520-1, P.; fig. pl, lxxv, 11, P. [E. F. C.]

Pinnularia, Ll. & Hutt; rootlet. C. M. Salisbury, from East Providence. ['87.]

Cordaiteæ.

Cordaites borassifolius, (St.) Unger, descr. pp. 532-3, P.; fig. pl. lxxvi, 3, 3*b*, P.

Cordaites diversifolius, Lesqx., descr. pp. 535-6. P.; fig. pl. lxxvii. 3, 3*a*, P.

Cordaites serpens, Lesqx., descr. pp. 542-3. P.; fig. pl. lxxix, 1-4, P. [E. F. C.]

Cordaites costatus? Lesqx., descr. p. 540-1. P.; fig. pl. lxxx, 1-3, and lxxxvi, 1, 2, P. E. F. Clark, from Bristol. ['87.] Not certain, nerves obsolete.

Fruits or Seeds.

Rhabdocarpus multistriatus, (St.) Presl, descr. p. 578, P.; fig. pl. lxxxv, 22, 23, P. E. F. Clark, from Newport. ['87.]

Rhabdocarpus clavatus, (St.) Gein., descr. p. 581, P.; fig. pl. lxxxv, 14, 20, P. E. F. Clark, from Bristol. ['87.]

Trigonocarpus species, a genus of fruit, descr. pp. 584-593 and 819-823, P. [C. H. H.]

Marine Plant.

Palæophycus Milleri, Lesqx., deser. p. 10, P.; fig. pl. A, 8–8*b*, P. [E. F. C.]

The above list contains one hundred and thirty-three species of fossil plants, of which eighty-three are ferns. This does not include synonyms, and species mentioned only in the notes.

Paleozoic Fauna of Rhode Island.

Mylacris Packardii, Scud. [A fossil insect found at Bristol, by E. F. Clark.]

Lingula prima. } [Fall River, Newport, etc., W. B. Rogers
Lingula antiqua. }   and others.]

Scolithus linearis. [Newport, W. O. Crosby.]

The four species named above have all been found in Carboniferous rocks; but the last three in pebbles which are fragments of much older rock, perhaps as old as the Potsdam sandstone, of Lower Silurian or Cambrian age. [See pp. 18, 26, 31, 43, 48, 49, 51, 55, of this report.] In the later editions of his works, Dana has substituted *Lingulella* for *Lingula.*

IV. CATALOGUE OF MINERALS FOUND IN RHODE ISLAND.

NATIVE SULPHUR, Cumberland, in cavities, probably from decomposed pyrite. Also found by Webb, attached to lime rock, Smithfield, in 1821, *Amer. Journ. Science*, vol. 4, p. 285.

NOTE. Many of the minerals mentioned in this list have been collected by members of this committee. The names and localities of others have been furnished by gentlemen well acquainted with the minerals of Rhode Island, or taken from Dana, Robinson, Jackson, the American Journal of Science, and other publications mentioned on the previous pages of this Report.

So many changes have been made in the towns of the State within the last half century, that it is difficult to give localities with exactness. This is specially true of Smithfield, from which Lincoln, North Smithfield, and a portion of Woonsocket have been taken, leaving the present Smithfield small in area. The other portion of Woonsocket has been taken from Cumberland; Pawtucket and East Providence, as Rhode Island towns, have been created within that period; Providence and Pawtucket have absorbed a large part of North Providence; a part of

MOLYBDENITE,—*Molybdenum Sulphide.*—Cumberland, Scituate, Westerly.

GRAPHITE,— *Plumbago,*— Portsmouth. Cranston. Cumberland (Valley Falls), Providence, Warwick, Jamestown.

GOLD, Johnston.

SILVER, Johnston, Lincoln (near Sayles' Bleachery). Also found in Cumberland, in 1778. [See p. 2 of this Report.]

CHALCOPYRITE,— *Copper Pyrites,*—Johnston, Portsmouth, Cumberland, Lincoln.

BORNITE,— *Variegated Copper Pyrites,*—Johnston, Cumberland.

MALACHITE and AZURITE,— *Green* and *Blue Copper Carbonate,*— Cumberland, Johnston.

GALENITE,— *Galena,*— Lincoln, Cumberland, Johnston.

RUTILE,—*Titanium Oxide,*—Johnston (Elm Farm), Woonsocket; in quartz crystals, Newport.

OCTAHEDRITE,— *Titanium Oxide,*— Cumberland (Poker Hill, near Ashton), Lincoln (Dexter Lime Rock).

PYRITE,—*Iron Pyrites,*—Newport, Bristol, Johnston, Cranston, Portsmouth, Lincoln, Valley Falls, Cumberland, Scituate: *radiated,* Johnston ; *cubo-octahedrons,* Lincoln, Johnston ; *dodecahedrons,* Lincoln.

ARSENOPYRITE,— *mispickel,*—Cumberland (Calumet Hill).

HEMATITE, Cranston, Cumberland, Valley Falls, Scituate ; *Specular Iron,* Cumberland, Cranston, Johnston, Foster ; *micaceous,* Johnston, Providence, Cumberland : *stalactitic, mammillary,* and *botryoidal,* Cumberland (Diamond Hill) ; *red ochre,* Cranston, Scituate, Cumberland ; *red chalk,* Providence : *clay iron stone,* Newport, Block Island.

Cranston has been annexed to Providence; and other changes have been made. The villages of Valley Falls, Ashton, and Manville are partly in Cumberland and partly in Lincoln; Pawtuxet is partly in Warwick and partly in Cranston; and other villages are similarly divided.

MENACCANITE,— *Ilmenite*,— *Titanic Hematite*,— Westerly, Woonsocket, Johnston.

MAGNETITE,—*Magnetic Iron Ore*,—Cumberland, Johnston, Scituate, Newport, Glocester; *octahedral*, Cumberland, Johnston, Smithfield, Glocester, Middletown; *sand*, Block Island, Westerly, the shores of Narragansett Bay, Providence (artesian well); *porphyritic, chrysolitic,* or *peridotyte*, Cumberland (Iron Mine Hill), and boulders to the south of it [see pp. 23, 44 of this Report], *titaniferous*, with a trace of manganese [pp. 42, 43, 52, 53, Jackson's Report]. Robinson, in 1825, had visited thirteen "mine holes" in the town of Cumberland, from most of which magnetite was obtained.

LIMONITE,—*Brown Hematite*,—Block Island, Foster, Cranston, Providence, Cumberland, Lincoln; *geodes*, Warwick; *yellow ochre*, Johnston, Cranston, Cumberland, Newport; *bog iron*, Warwick, Cranston, Narragansett Pier, Foster, Block Island, Providence, Cumberland.

MELANTERITE,—*Copperas*,—*Iron Vitriol*,—Cranston, Block Island, Cumberland, Foster, Newport Neck.

SIDERITE,—*Spathic Iron*,—North Smithfield, Cumberland, Portsmouth, Jamestown; in steatite, Johnston; radiate nodules in quartz, Jamestown.

PYROLUSITE,—*Black Oxide of Manganese*,—Cumberland, "E. side of Blackstone River, $2\frac{1}{2}$ miles N. of Pawtucket."

FLUORITE,—*Fluor Spar;* chlorophane, purple, blue, green, and white, Cumberland; purple, perhaps chlorophane, found by Webb, in 1821, in Seekonk, now East Providence; also Providence [Robinson]; traces in flinty slate, Newport Neck [Dale]; Woonsocket, Westerly.

GYPSUM, crystals, in iron ore, from pyrite, Newport Neck.

APATITE, Cumberland (Diamond Hill).

CALCITE,—*Calc Spar*,—Lincoln* (Lime Rock, Harris and Dexter quarries), Cumberland, Johnston, Pawtucket, Central

---

* The town of Lincoln was set off from Smithfield in 1871; hence the limestone quarries and the village of Lime Rock are now in Lincoln, instead of Smithfield.

Falls, Scituate, North Smithfield, Westerly, Newport (Castle Hill), Portsmouth; *nail-head* and *dog-tooth spar*, Lincoln; *Iceland*, or *double-refraction spar*, Lincoln; *blue*, Lincoln, Cumberland; *argentine*, Lincoln; *travertine*, Cumberland: *limestone*, white, yellow, blue, variegated, and *dentritic* (formation of manganese), Lincoln, North Providence; *marble*, or *granular limestone*, Johnston, North Providence, Cranston; black and white, Lincoln; green and white, Cumberland.

DOLOMITE; *Rhomb*, *brown*, and *bitter spar*, Lincoln, Cumberland, Johnston; *pearl spar*, Lincoln, Johnston; *dendritic*, Lincoln; *magnesian limestone*, Lincoln, Newport, Johnston, etc.

Quartz.

Drusy Quartz, Cumberland (Diamond Hill).

Rock Crystal, Cumberland*, Lincoln (Lime Rock), Newport, Middletown, Coventry, North Providence; curved crystals, Providence, Lime Rock.

Amethyst, Bristol, Cumberland, Westerly, Burrillville; also on banks of the Blackstone river, in Cumberland, probably washed several miles from its gangue.

Rose Quartz, Cumberland, Lincoln.

*Citrine,—False Topaz,—*Foster, Glocester, Pawtuxet, Lincoln, Cumberland.

Smoky Quartz, Cumberland, Pawtucket, Coventry, Scituate, Lincoln, Johnston.

Milky Quartz, Bristol (Mount Hope), Cumberland, Smithfield, East Greenwich, Providence, Newport, Middletown, Jamestown.

Greasy Quartz, Cumberland.

Cat's Eye? Cumberland.

Prase, Cumberland.

Blue Quartz, Providence, Smithfield.

---

* Most of the Cumberland localities for Quartz are at Diamond Hill.

Ferruginous Quartz, Diamond Hill, East Greenwich.

Massive Quartz, throughout the State; *granular*, Cranston, North Smithfield (Woonsocket Hill), Cumberland, Jamestown; *fibrous*, Central Falls, Cranston; *stalactitic*, Lime Rock; *cellular*, Lincoln; *babel* and *radiated*, Diamond Hill.

Geodes, Burrillville.

Fetid Quartz, Cumberland, Pawtuxet, Cranston.

Pseudomorphous Quartz, Cumberland.

Thetis Hair Stone. "quartz penetrated by delicate green crystals of actinolite," Cumberland.

Sagenitic Quartz, penetrated by black hornblende, actinolite, or asbestus, Cumberland, Cranston, Middletown; by rutile, Middletown; by graphite and pyrite, Cranston.

Quartz Crystals containing pearl spar, Cumberland and Lincoln (Dexter Lime Rock); containing chlorite, Cumberland; containing siderite, Jamestown; containing dendrite, Lincoln (Dexter Lime Rock).

Chalcedony, Diamond Hill, Johnston, Providence; *botryoidal*, Lincoln; *mammillary*, pale blue, on quartz, Burrillville.

Carnelian, Westerly, Warwick (Pawtuxet).

Agate, Bristol, Diamond Hill, "composed of quartz, jasper, chalcedony, and hornstone, variously disposed in stripes, spots, or irregular figures"; *fortification* and *ribbon* agate, Diamond Hill.

Jasper, Bristol, Providence, Pawtucket, Pawtuxet, Newport, Westerly, Little Compton; flesh-colored, red, yellow, brown, blue, green, and grey, eyed and striped. Diamond Hill, Cumberland.

Hornstone, Cumberland, Cranston.

Basanite,—*Lydian stone*,—*touchstone*,— found in Newport, by Taylor and Webb, in 1824.

OPAL; *opalized quartz?* Cumberland; *infusorial earth.* North Providence, Cumberland; *cacholong.* Diamond Hill [Jackson].

PYROXENE; *Augite*, Scituate, Middletown; *Sahlite*, Cumberland [Jackson].

RHODONITE,—*Red Silicate of Manganese*; *Photicite*, Cumberland.

Amphibole,— Hornblende.

Tremolite, Lincoln (fine white), Cumberland (Tower Hill), Johnston, North Providence, Cranston; *fibrous*, Cranston, Lime Rock, Johnston, East Providence; *stellated* and *radiated*, Lime Rock, Cumberland; *glassy*, Johnston.

Actinolite, Lincoln (Manville), Cumberland, Johnston, Cranston, Foster, Coventry; crystals in steatite and slate, Johnston, Cranston; *glassy*, Johnston; *ligneous*, Cumberland.

Asbestus, Lincoln, Cumberland, Bristol, Johnston, Newport, Cranston, East Greenwich; silicated curved, Cranston; green, Cumberland, Lincoln, Cranston, Portsmouth; yellow, Cranston, Johnston; brown, Cumberland; *radiated*, Jamestown; *amianthus*, Lincoln, Johnston, Cumberland, Providence; *ligniform*, Cumberland, Smithfield; *mountain leather*, Lincoln, Cranston.

Hornblende, black, Cumberland, Providence, Johnston, Woonsocket, Cranston; green, Providence, Johnston; *radiated* and *acicular* crystals in slate, Johnston, Cumberland; *fasciculite*, Johnston, Woonsocket.

CROCIDOLITE,—*Blue Asbestus*,—Cumberland.

BERYL, Westerly, Smithfield, Cumberland, North Providence, Foster.

CHRYSOLITE,—*Olivine*,—Cumberland.

KNEBELITE, Cumberland; the "ferro-silicate of manganese," p. 7 of this Report. [Jackson's Report, pp. 54, 55.]

GARNET, Cranston, Smithfield, Jamestown; precious, Foster, Natick, Block Island; red, Natick, Foster, Johnston, Westerly, Block Island, Scituate, Cumberland; brown and cinnamon, Cumberland ; green (poor), Cumberland ; massive, Johnston, Cumberland.

EPIDOTE, Providence, Cumberland, Newport, Johnston, Lincoln, Jamestown (near Dumplings).

ZOISITE, Cumberland, Woonsocket, Middletown (Paradise), Smithfield (probably Lincoln) ; *saussurite*, Lincoln (Lime Rock) [Emmons].

ILVAITE.— *Yenite*,—*Lievrite*,—Cumberland (Tower Hill). [See pp. 4, 5 of this Report.] Much of the so-called yenite recently found in Cumberland is knebelite ; but true yenite has also been found there within a few years.

MICAS,—BIOTITE and MUSCOVITE,—are found as constituents of the granite, gneiss, and mica schists of the State, affording some very good specimens for the cabinet ; black, transparent, yellowish green, Cranston, Smithfield, Coventry, Glocester, Westerly, Cumberland, Block Island, etc. ; two species, crystals. Middletown (Paradise), South Kingstown (Watson's Pier) [Dale] ; black, hexagonal crystals, Scituate ; *tufted*, Foster ; *nacrite*, on quartz and calcite, Lincoln (Dexter Lime Rock).

FELDSPARS,—*triclinic* and *monoclinic*,—are found in different parts of the State, as constituents of granite, gneiss, and other rocks, often quite coarsely crystallized ; but little seems to have been done to determine the species. Crystals have been found in Scituate, Smithfield, Middletown (Paradise), Newport, Westerly, etc. The feldspar of the Cumberland iron ore is *triclinic* or *plagioclase ;* MICROCLINE, or *Chesterlite,* is found in Lincoln (Dexter Lime Rock) ; ORTHOCLASE in Westerly, Scituate, and Cumberland ; blue in Glocester ; flesh-colored in Hopkinton ; perhaps also LABRADORITE and other species, as constituents of the rocks of the State.

TOURMALINE, black, Scituate, Coventry, Woonsocket, Johnston, Cumberland, Smithfield.

CYANITE,—*Kyanite*,—Foster, Cumberland, Cranston, Woonsocket.

TITANITE,—*Sphene.*—found by Webb in Seekonk (East Providence), in 1821–2, "near the fluor rock."

STAUROLITE.—*Staurotide*,—Conanicut Island (Jamestown).

STILBITE, fibrous, Woonsocket.

TALC, *green*, Cumberland, North Providence, Johnston, North Smithfield, Foster, Lincoln, Coventry, Newport, Middletown; *columnar*, Cumberland, Johnston; *foliated*, Johnston, North Smithfield; *white*, Lincoln (Lime Rock); *steatite,—soapstone,—*Johnston, Cranston, North Smithfield, Lincoln, North Providence, Cumberland; *French chalk*, Johnston; *indurated*, Johnston; *dendritic*, Lincoln (Dexter Lime Rock).

SERPENTINE. Newport, Cumberland, Johnston, Lincoln, Providence; *Bowenite*, formerly called *nephrite*, Lincoln (Harris Lime Rock); *Chrysotile*, Cumberland, Newport Neck; *Baltimorite*, Cumberland; *Picrolite*, Lincoln, Newport Neck [Dale].

KAOLINITE, Woonsocket, Burrillville, Lincoln.

CHLORITES, Johnston, Lincoln, Woonsocket, Foster, Jamestown, Westerly, Cumberland, Pawtucket, Providence, Middletown (Paradise). Newport (Castle Hill and Rose Island); partial pseudomorphs after garnet and staurolite, Conanicut Island, northern part, west side [Dale].

CHLORITOID; *Masonite*, Warwick (Natick village); *Phyllite*, Cumberland, Providence, Newport, Cranston; *Newportite*, Newport; *Ottrelite*, Jamestown [Dale].

MINERAL COAL; *Anthracite*, Portsmouth, Newport, Cranston, Cumberland (Valley Falls), Providence, Warwick; *Lignite*, Block Island; *Peat*, Johnston, Block Island, Cumberland, Providence, North Providence, Woonsocket, Cranston, Bristol, North Kingstown, South Kingstown, Wickford, Warwick, Pawtuxet. [Analyses, p. 245, J.]

V. LIST OF LOCALITIES IN RHODE ISLAND OF INTEREST TO THE GEOLOGIST AND MINERALOGIST.

Cumberland.

This town has been styled "the mineral pocket of New England." E. Hitchcock called it "one of the most metalliferous spots in New England." As will be seen from the preceding catalogue, most of the rarer minerals found in the State occur in this town.

Diamond Hill and vicinity, noted for the various forms of quartz, hematite, galena, apatite, etc., pp. 51, 52, Jackson.

Diamond Hill Granite Quarry (on the east side of *Calumet Hill*) and *Beacon Pole Hill* [556 feet above the sea], hornblende gneiss or syenitic granite, arsenopyrite, epidote, tremolite, magnetite, fluor-spar, etc.

Cumberland Hill, Sneech Pond, and *Copper Mine Hill,* limestone and dolomite [analyses, p. 246, J.], various copper and iron ores and forms of hornblende, chlorite, epidote, steatite, prase, thetis hair stone and other forms of quartz, fluor-spar, garnet, molybdenite, photicite, yenite, knebelite [analysis, pp. 54, 55, J.]. Jackson states that "there are no less than fifty different ancient mine holes in this hill." They run from the south side of Sneech Pond around the east side of the pond to Tower Hill, which lies between Sneech Pond on the south and Beacon Pole Hill on the north.

Iron Mine Hill, porphyritic titaniferous magnetite, olivine, serpentine, feldspar, etc. Jackson gives a section of the hill and analysis of the ore, pp. 52, 53; also states facts as to the boulders carried south, and scratches, pp. 42, 43. See pp. 23, 44 of this Report.

Valley Falls, coal mine, fossil plants, graphite, anthracite [analysis p. 239, J.], pyrolusite.

NOTE. Many of these localities have been referred to on the previous pages of this Report. Sources of information concerning them will be found in the Index, when not here mentioned. The references marked J. are to Jackson's Report on the Geological Survey of Rhode Island.

Woonsocket.

Scythe Stone Quarries. Jackson, p. 70, gives a section showing conglomerate resting upon and passing into mica slate, with boulders upon the surface. Ten thousand dozen whetstones were manufactured in 1839.

North Smithfield.

Woonsocket Hill, 576 feet above the sea, probably the highest point in the State; granular quartz, mica, talc; old quarry for hearthstones, etc.

Lincoln.

Harris Lime Rock and *Middle Lime Rock*, various forms of calcite and dolomite [analyses, p. 246, J.], dendrites, quartz crystals, stalactitic quartz, white talc, tremolite, Bowenite, etc. Jackson gives a section and sketch, pp. 58, 59. This limestone was used, in 1822, for the trimmings of Hope College, Brown University.

Dexter Lime Rock and vicinity, various forms of calcite and dolomite [analyses, p. 246, J.], dendrites, quartz crystals, white talc, pyrite, steatite, nacrite, etc. Pp. 66–69, J. Jackson [pp. 35, 68], says that the rhomb spar of the Lime Rocks contains manganese, but does not give it in his printed analysis of limestones.

Both the Harris and the Dexter rocks are said to have been worked soon after the first settlement of the colony, in the time of Roger Williams. Jackson states that, of the lime made at the Dexter rock, 10,000 casks were annually sold, from 1800 to 1840.

Arnold's, or *Smithfield. Ledge*, on the west bank of the Moshassuck river, from which granitic stone with natural faces was taken for St. John's Church, Providence, in 1811, and St. Stephen's Church, in 1861.

Arnold's Quarry, near the Butterfly Factory, from which limestone for asphalt pavement was taken, serpentine, picrolite.

Scott's Pond, floating island.

Johnston.

Snake Den Ledge, in the northerly part of the town. This region contains six or more parallel ridges running north and south. The principal valley has a high, steep ledge on the east, about 150 feet high, and perhaps 300 feet above the level of the sea, with loose, angular boulders thickly strewn over its side, so that it is difficult to find the parent ledge. The fragments are of all sizes, and most of them have apparently been taken right from the ledge. On the west of this valley the hill is only some 50 feet high, with few boulders and the ledge well smoothed and rounded, evidently by glacial action, but with only obscure striation, on account of the character of the rocks and their exposure to atmospheric action. The rock on both sides of the valley is apparently of the same varieties as the Round Rocks boulders, granitic and gneissoid, of varying composition and structure. The dip on the ridges west of the principal valley is to the east, in all cases seen, varying from about 30° to nearly vertical. The dip of the rocks east of that valley was not satisfactorily determined, but may be to the south.

The stone for the First Congregational Church, Providence, is said to have been brought from this ledge, in 1816. Johnston formerly supplied much granite for building purposes.

Round Rocks, in the south-westerly part of the town, about three miles south of Snake Den. A great collection of boulders, of all sizes, from a few pounds in weight up to twelve or fifteen feet in diameter. They are in places heaped so closely together that trees can hardly grow between them, but other parts were well wooded at the time of our visits. Some of the rock is disintegrating, and much of the soil is evidently made of this decaying rock. The boulders cover an area extending perhaps a quarter of a mile in length and a few hundred feet in width. This is one of the best illustrations in the State of boulders transported by glacial action from the north. The rock is like that found at Snake Den and other ledges to the north, granitic and gneissoid.

Bear Rock, in the north-easterly part of the town, from which the granite columns of the Providence Arcade were taken, in 1828.

Brown's Lime Quarry, said to have been first worked for lime by Stephen Hopkins, about the middle of the last century. Jackson gives a section, p. 80, analysis, p. 246. Green acicular and fasiculated actinolite, octahedral magnetite, chlorite, green talc, etc. On Manton road, N. of Elm Farm.

Jenkins' Lime Quarry, granular limestone [section p. 81, analysis p. 246, J.], serpentine, steatite, etc. On "Almy Farm." Hartford pike, W. of Elm Farm.

Indian Ledge and *Mineral Spring* (Elm Farm), green talc, rutile, menaccanite, steatite or soapstone, some of it containing siderite and limestone; a place where Indian pottery was manufactured. On Hartford pike.

Thurber's Ledge, from which the stone of some Providence buildings was taken. In northern part of the town.

Neutakonkanut Hill [296 feet above the sea]. Jackson, p. 82, gives a view of a boulder of hornblende rock resting upon mica slate, on the south side of the hill, carried there from the north, by glacial action; micaceous iron, north end of hill; glacial striae, Hartford pike.

Providence.

Mount Pleasant, glacial striae on the top, and on the east side, near Atwell's Avenue [see p. 40 of this Report]; phyllite.

Prospect Hill, *College Hill*, and the *East Side*, fossil plants, graphite, and anthracite [analysis p. 239, J.]; also serpentine and fluor-spar were found 60 or more years since.

Smith's Hill, modified drift, a deposit of sand and gravel perhaps 70 feet deep. Most of the *West Side* of the city is of the same character.

Field's Point presents hills of gravel and sand whose peculiar rounded backs and hollows, as well as boulders, show that they were deposited by glaciers.

East Providence.

Silver Spring, fossil plants and glacial marks.

Ide's Ledge and ledge near *Hunt's Mill*, fossil plants (calamites), milky quartz, graywacke or fine conglomerate, with natural faces, used for buildings in Providence.

Cranston.

Iron Mine, opened in 1762 by Gov. Hopkins, and worked until 1780, hematite, limonite, etc.

Coal Mine, Sockanosset, fossil plants, graphite, anthracite, phyllite, remarkable spring, pp. 85, 86, 203, J.

Fenner's Ledge, Durfee's Ledge, and *Harris Ledge*, fossil plants, asbestus, phyllite, conglomerate, "mica-schist" used for foundations of buildings in Providence.

Warwick.

Natick, boulders of Masonite, description and analysis, pp. 87, 88, J.

Warwick Neck, fossil plants, graphite, anthracite, mineral spring, pp. 83, 84, J.

Apponaug, Drum Rock, a rocking stone, description and view, pp. 84, 85, J. A better description and cut are referred to on p. 5 of this Report.

South Kingstown.

Tower Hill [160 feet above the sea], plumbago, p. 89, J.

Wolf Rocks, partly in this town and partly in Exeter. A ravine about an eighth of a mile long and fifty feet deep, running northwest and southeast, and cutting across a long ridge or hill. The sides, especially on the north, are covered with large boulders, some of them ten or twelve feet in diameter. These boulders are not much rounded, and have not travelled far, evidently having been brought from the north by glacial action. Some of them are of coarse granite, containing flesh-colored feldspar; in others the feldspar is whitish; many are of dark gneiss; and one, at least, is of white quartz.

Terminal Moraine. A reference to pages 37–39, 46, 47 of this Report will show that a glacial terminal moraine is supposed to run through South Kingstown, Charlestown, and Westerly, and possibly an intermediate one through South Kingstown and North Kingstown.

Money Stone. One or more rocks bearing this name have been observed in South Kingstown or Charlestown. A piece of a boulder so named, said to be from Charlestown, near the Sound, is a conglomerate with the pebbles much metamorphosed, the center of each pebble being different in color from the outside,—a kind of concretionary conglomerate.

Westerly.

Granite Quarries and vicinity, feldspar crystals, micas, quartz, amethyst, pyrite, ilmenite, beryl, garnet. In the Tenth U. S. Census, vol. x, is a chromolithograph of " Biotite Granite, Westerly, R. I.," plate xxxix. In the same volume, under the head of " Microscopic Structure," G. P. Merrill says: "The granites of Westerly, R. I., are biotitic, but differ from those just mentioned in being usually of a finer texture and more rich in accessory minerals, containing frequently small crystals of fluor-spar, sphene, menaccanite, magnetite, apatite, epidote, and pyrite; the quartz contains also many of the small, thread-like crystals so characteristic of rutile. Many of the Westerly granites are of a flesh-red color, but otherwise than this they do not differ materially from the ordinary gray granites, the red color being, as usual, due to the red orthoclase they contain." These granites are very extensively used, not only in Providence, but in other parts of the country.

Bristol.

Poppasquash Neck and *Bristol Neck*, fossil plants, glacial scratches, pp. 104, 105, J.

Bristol Ferry, amethyst, pyrite.

Mount Hope, white quartz and quartz crystals [view p. 79, J.], glacial scratches.

Portsmouth.

Coal Mines, siderite crystals, fossil plants, graphite, anthracite. Description and analyses, pp. 95-104, 239, 240, J., and colored section. Jackson and later authorities refer to the large proportion of water in the coal. See p. 54, this Report.

Prudence Island, fossil plants, sand drifts.

Middletown.

Purgatory, about which much has been written, as the Index of this Report will show. The elongation of the pebbles in the conglomerate, their parallel arrangement, and the clearly cut sets of parallel planes of division are the chief points of interest. An examination of the foregoing pages of this Report, will show that the theory of plasticity after the conglomerate was formed has of late years been the one commonly accepted. Jackson and other early authorities stated that the chasm "was once filled by a dyke of greenstone trap, which has been worn away," "a small portion only remaining in the south end of the rent, to attest its former presence." W. B. Rogers, in 1875, said, the chasm "has been erroneously regarded as due to the decay of a dyke of trap, supposed to have occupied the cavity." Pp. 93, 94, J. Magnetite crystals.

Paradise, Hanging Rock, conglomerate and other rocks, about which different opinions have prevailed, as shown in the preceding pages of this Report, and pp. 93, 94, J.; chlorite, feldspar crystals, mica crystals, magnetite crystals, zoisite.

Wood's Castle, fossil plants, white on black ground.

Sachuest Neck and *Point*, fossil plants, milky quartz, talc.

Quartz crystals penetrated by acicular crystals of rutile and hornblende have recently been found in Middletown, near Newport,— those with actinolite, at least, "in a quartz vein of the conglomerate of the Carboniferous series" [Dale].

Newport.

Miantonomah Hill, section, p. 92, J.

Newport Neck. anthracite, fossil plants, clay iron stone, pyrite, jasper, feldspar crystals, chrysotile, picrolite, green and purple serpentine, talc, epidote, yellow ochre, pp. 89-91, J. Limestone near Fort Adams, analysis, p. 246, J.

Lime Islands, in the harbor, description and analysis, pp. 91, 92, 246, J.

Jamestown.

West shore of Conanicut Island. "$4\frac{1}{2}$ miles from the north end and $5\frac{3}{4}$ miles from the south end of the island," staurolite and garnets; also chlorite (partial pseudomorphs), ottrelite. [Robinson and Dale.]

Dumplings and *Mackerel Cove*, siderite, epidote; also pyrite crystals, South Conanicut [Dale].

Block Island.

A portion of the glacial terminal moraine, clay, boulders, iron sand, bog iron ore, lignite, peat.

Miscellaneous.

"Devil's foot marks," near Wickford, description and cut, pp. 86, 87, J.

Balanced rock, farm of E. S. Thurber, North Providence.

Direction of glacial scratches, p. 43, J.

Pawtucket has furnished fossil plants. Those from Mansfield, Wrentham, and adjacent portions of Massachusetts belong to the same formation as those of Rhode Island.

"Nipmuck granite" has been quarried in South Scituate [p. 76, J.] or Coventry. It is a gneiss which has been much used in Providence, for crossings, flags, and buildings, distinguished from others by its yellow look, has "quite a large proportion of muscovite, with much less biotite, in layers, and hence splits quite smoothly." Pascoag gneiss has also been used in Providence.

Octahedral magnetite has been found in Glocester, farm of Daniel Tucker.

Wallum Pond, Burrillville, a beautiful sheet of clear water, in the north-western part of Rhode Island, extending into Massachusetts. On its shores are many boulders, especially on the southern and western sides, with woods of pine and oak.

Jackson [p. 216] gives analysis of limestone from quarry in North Providence. There are also quarries of other stone in the portion of North Providence annexed to the city of Providence, Whelden's and other ledges.

There have been attempts to mine gold in different parts of the State, but with little success.

VI. Results obtained by Digging and Boring in Rhode Island.

A map of the city of Providence and vicinity, prepared for us in the office of the city engineer, is marked to show where the ledge is known to lie near the surface. The map indicates the localities of surface rock; also where the ledge has been struck at a depth of five feet in laying water pipes, and ten or twelve feet in constructing sewers. We have also made inquiries of those who have been engaged in digging for building operations, or sinking artesian wells, and present in this portion of the Report such facts as we have been able to gather. We suggest that more care should be taken to collect and preserve such information; and, where it is possible, specimens of rock encountered at different depths, properly labeled, should be somewhere preserved. When not otherwise indicated, the particulars in regard to artesian borings have, in most cases, been furnished, from memory, by Mr. D. L. Barker.

In the greater portion of the East Side of Providence, the ledge lies quite near the surface. It is found at the surface on the corner of Gano and George streets, the corner of Prospect and Barnes streets, on the south side of Cypress street near Camp street, and other places. It has frequently been struck in water and sewer trenches in the area extending from North street on the north to Waterman street on the south, and from Benefit and North Main streets on the west to East avenue and Brook street on the east. In most of Congdon street and a large part of Camp street, the bed-rock lies within five feet of the surface; and the same is true of portions of Prospect street and various other streets. The northeast corner of Hope reservoir was blasted from the solid rock. In nearly the whole of Olney street, from North Main street to the point where it turns to the north, the ledge lies within twelve feet of the surface. In fact, the rock has already been found within that distance of the surface in about thirty streets within the area named above; also in the whole of Governor street north of Power street, in Manning street between Governor and Gano streets, in Gano street between Manning and Pitman streets, and at one point in Taber avenue just north of Humboldt avenue. The rock on which Roger Williams is said to have landed was a ledge on the bank of the Seekonk river, near the corner of Williams and Gano streets. It has recently been covered with sand and gravel; but detached portions of the rock have been raised to the present level.

The underlying rock of the East Side is of the Carboniferous age, in some places graywacke conglomerate, and in others carboniferous shale or slate, often with fossil plants. The two kinds of rock are sometimes found in the same street. In digging for the sewer on Benefit street, very hard graywacke was found north of the man-hole between Church and Starr streets; but south of that point was found slate, with plumbago, coal, and asbestus. In most of the streets, however, the rock is black slate or shale, and not graywacke. The dip is thought, by those who work upon the sewers, to be about forty-five degrees, a little north of east, in all the region above described.

The material above the ledge is found to differ widely in different portions of the East Side. So far as we have been able to trace it, a division line runs approximately as follows: Commencing near the corner of John and Brook streets, running along John, Governor, Power, Ives, Amy, and Gano streets to Angell street, thence north-easterly (crossing Humboldt avenue between Elmgrove and Wayland avenues) to Butler avenue, thence northerly along that avenue, and turning again to the north-east, striking the river on the grounds of the Butler Hospital, near Swan Point. To the north and west of this line is found "hard-pan,"— apparently both lower and upper till; that is, the unmodified drift, just as it was left by the glacier, including the ground moraine and the material which the glacier deposited at melting; mingled clay, sand, boulders, and angular stones, often almost as hard to dig as a solid ledge would be, sometimes called "marl." Various colors are found, red (apparently from the red rock to the north), yellow, gray, black, and bluish tints. Water is usually reached near the surface. To the south and east of this line is found a deep deposit of modified drift,—stratified sand and fine gravel, evidently deposited by water,—easily dug, with water far below the surface. In John street, however, sand extends only about twelve feet below the surface, after which clay is found.

The plane dividing these widely different classes of material is perfectly distinct, and it generally seems to be nearly vertical. The surface of the ground usually presents no indication of its existence, though the area of modified drift is dry and perhaps more nearly level, where it has not been washed away by the recent flow of water; while the surface of the unmodified drift is more rounded in outline, with springs and swampy regions. Apparently the ice of the glacier was washed away on the side towards the Seekonk river, the flood carrying with it the deposit of till; and subsequently the water deposited there the sand and fine gravel, while the ice still remained on the area of unmodified drift.

An artesian well, sunk near the corner of Angell and Wayland streets, shows the character of this area of modified drift. Dr. W. M. Jackson gives the strata as follows, beginning at the surface:

White sand, moderately fine, . . 35 feet.
Quick-sand, very fine and white, . . 25 "
Black sand, largely magnetic, . . 2 "
Blue clay, dense and compact, . . 8 "
Blue gravel, very coarse, . . . 4 " 7 inches.

The bed-rock was struck at seventy-four feet and seven inches from the surface, which is just about the level of the sea. No boulders were encountered. The ledge shelved at quite a sharp angle toward the river, and the pipe was so bent by driving against the ledge that dynamite cartridges were used to blow off the end. Quite a cavity was thus made in the ledge, and many fragments of it were brought up. The rock was of slate, but many pieces " had an admixture of quartz with the slate—a silvery, glassy white quartz—not mineral bearing." Dr. Jackson "judged the ledge to be slate, with an accidental quartz leader beneath the pipe opening." The water above the black sand was " unusually hard and unfit to drink;" that in the blue gravel, between the blue clay and bed-rock, was " first class in every particular," and " appeared to fill the four foot seven inch space."

In the south-western and extreme southern portion of the East Side, the ledge does not lie very near the surface. None was encountered, south of Angell street, in digging for the Brook street sewer; but indications of a beach (broken shells, pebbles, etc.) were found between Pike and Tockwotton streets. In boring a well at the Tool Company's works (now Household Sewing Machine Company), on the western part of Wickenden street, in 1866, before Mr. Barker began his work, the ledge was struck at perhaps 35 feet below the surface, and the boring continued to a depth of about 270 feet. Coal was found which was burned in the company's fires. About 1880, other wells were started on these premises, which struck solid rock at about 12, 22, and 40 feet. None of the wells were successful in supplying water. Probably the rock at 12 feet, under the building, was a boulder, as there was an old well near by, dug 30 feet deep. The ledge seems to be further from the surface towards the river. It is said that rock, either boulder or ledge, was struck 12 or 15 feet below the surface, in a well between South Main and Well streets, near Williams street.

A hill of loose material, gravel and sand, between Fox Point and India Point, has been removed within a few years, and used for the streets and for filling the flats of the Seekonk river in the vicinity of Roger Williams Rock, and other low places on the East Side. There was formerly a pond, south of Wickenden street, into which the brook of Brook street flowed. The outlet of the pond was into the Providence river, near the present location of the works of the Providence Steam Engine Company.

In the office of the city engineer is the record of six test wells, sunk in 1882, under the new Washington bridge over the Seekonk river, near India Point. The most western one, sunk where the water was then the deepest, west of the present draw, differs from all the others. It was carried only 84 feet below high water, and passed through about 30 feet of water, 16 feet of mud, and 38 feet of gravel. The others were carried from 98 to 108 feet below high water. Two of them struck a slate rock, probably the ledge, at 96 and 106 feet; but the others did not. In all the wells, immediately below the water of the river was a layer of mud and oyster shells, or clayey mud, from 16 to 34 feet thick; and in all except the two eastern ones, which were not in the deep water in the middle of the river, the mud terminated about 46 feet below high water. In all except the western one, which was about 125 feet from the next, there were various layers of fine and coarse sand and gravel, including a layer of quick-sand 20 to 30 feet thick, but very little clay. The layers of gravel were mostly from 2 to 12 feet thick, and in one of them there was a good supply of fresh water.

There are out-crops of the ledge near the city, at Kettle Point, Silver Spring, and other places in the town of East Providence.

Leaving the East Side, we find marked upon the map no other parts of the city where the ledge has been struck in digging for water pipes or sewers, except short distances at Atwell's avenue and Coville street, and Manton avenue and Aleppo street. In the un-sewered parts of the city, the ledge crops out in various places, especially in the extreme northern and north-western portions of the city, as at the ledges south of Windmill Hill, north of Geneva, near Eagle Park, Manton, Dyerville, Mount Pleasant, and various other places. Most of these ledges are from 100 to 200 feet above the level of the sea. The ledge also reaches the surface on the east side of Rocky Hill in Cranston, and in many places on Neutakonkanut Hill in Johnston, even on the summit, 296 feet high.

Smith's Hill and the West Side of the city proper consist of a great depth of modified drift, stratified sand, gravel, and clay, with no "hard pan" or ledge at ordinary depths.

The Silver Spring Bleaching and Dyeing Company's works are located in the northern part of the city, on Charles street north of the railroad crossing, where the ground is about 30 feet above the sea. About 30 wells, some flowing and others pumping, have been sunk there. Twenty-three of the pumping wells furnish more than 1,000 gallons of water per minute, running ten hours a day. Mr. Barker claims that these wells are the second best in the United States, so far as the volume of good water is concerned. One of the wells struck the ledge at about 155 feet from the surface, and went into the rock about 12 feet, when the tools were lost and the well abandoned. From the description, we suppose the ledge to be graywacke. The other wells are from 89 to 134 feet below the surface, most of them from 100 to 120 feet. The strata are mostly from 1 to 10 feet thick, and differ much in the different wells.— quick-sand, fine sand, and coarse sand, white, yellow, brown, grey, and black, with one layer of blue sand. There is no clay, and few layers of gravel, except at the bottom, where the water-bearing gravel is found. Within 50 feet of the surface the water contains iron, and is unfit for use.

In 1879-80, six wells were sunk on the premises of the R. I. Tool Company, West River street, where the present surface is also about 30 feet above the sea. They were carried to depths varying from 48 to 130 feet, without striking the ledge; and, together, by pumping, yield 152 gallons per minute.

In 1885, soundings were made by the city engineer, to a depth of 40 to 54 feet below high water, in order to determine the character of the underlying strata at five points: Crawford Street Bridge, Washington Row, outlet of the Cove, centre of the Cove, and entrance of Woonasquatucket river. The first stratum, in each case, was of mud, 8 to 15 feet thick; below that were found varying layers of sand and gravel, 1 to 11 feet thick, in most cases with a layer of gravel at the bottom of the boring. No amount of quick-sand was found, except layers 4 to 8 feet thick, at the two points last named above; and a layer of clay, 11 and 13 feet thick, was found only in the same two borings. Both the quick-sand and clay were apparently deposited where the water began to move more slowly on entering the Cove.

West of the Cove basin is found a peculiar stratum of ferruginous conglomerate, composed of pebbles from one to six inches in diameter, cemented together. It lies near the surface at the "vitriol" works, and from twelve to thirty feet below the surface under the building of the Brown and Sharpe Manufacturing Company, on Promenade street, where the surface is about 10 feet above the sea. The stratum of conglomerate is from six inches to four feet thick, with quick-sand both above and below it, while the ledge is perhaps 130 feet below the surface. Builders are careful to reach this conglomerate in driving piles and laying foundations, and equally careful not to break through this stratum.

At the Brown & Sharpe works are three wells, about 135 feet deep, in which the water stands about three feet below the sidewalk. The borings passed through various layers of sand, quick-sand, clay, "marl," and gravel; and two of them struck a slate rock, apparently the ledge.

NOTE.—Most of the particulars pertaining to the wells of the Silver Spring B. & D. Co., R. I. Tool Co., Brown & Sharpe Mfg. Co., and Nicholson File Co., have been obtained at the works, some of them from records kept there.

From 1879 to 1882, five flowing wells were bored by the Nicholson File Company, on Acorn street, also near the Woonasquatucket river, where the surface is about 10 feet above the sea. They are from 107 to 130 feet deep, without striking the ledge, and passed through blue clay and sand of different colors, with coarse sand and gravel at the bottom, which yields the water. One of the wells yields 30 gallons a minute.

The Richmond Manufacturing Company and the Providence Worsted Mills, Valley street; and the Valley Worsted Mills, Eagle street, have sunk wells, the latter one said to be 176 feet deep, yielding 40 gallons per minute. Most of the wells mentioned in this paragraph were sunk before 1879, when Mr. Barker commenced his work.

Five wells have been sunk on Aborn street, near Westminster street, on the West Side, south of the Cove basin, where the surface is less than 20 feet above the sea. The strata found were of sand, gravel, and cobble, without quicksand or clay of any amount. The ledge was reached at about 105 feet from the surface. Just above the ledge was a layer of gravel, some 30 feet thick, which furnished a good supply of water. One of the wells was carried into the solid rock about 50 feet, or 155 feet from the surface. The rock seemed to be about like that of Fenner's ledge, Cranston, of Carboniferous age.

At the Barstow Stove Foundry, foot of Chestnut street, near Point street, where the ground is about 10 feet above the sea, the ledge was reached at 65 feet below the surface, the last part, at least, through gravel mixed with clay, or "hard pan." The well was continued through the ledge of carboniferous shale and plumbago 140 feet, or 205 feet from the surface. In other wells in that vicinity, one of which was carried 230 feet below the surface, the ledge was also reached at about 65 feet, and was like that at Barstow's, only softer in some cases.

In 1885, six borings were made to test the foundation for the gas holder on Langley street, near Eddy street, where the surface is 8½ feet above high water. The strata encountered were about 10 feet of sand ; 1 to 2 feet of fine sand, mud, and water ; 10 to 14 feet of dock-mud or clay ; 3 to 5 feet of gravel or gravel sand, with flowing water. Underneath the gravel was clay, which was struck at a depth of 29 to 30 feet from the surface, and the " test-holes " were not continued further. In 1871, an artesian well a little over 300 feet deep was bored at this West station, on Langley street. It went through about 56½ feet of sand, mud, clay, and gravel ; 112 feet of slate and sandstone or conglomerate ; and 132 feet or more of granite and quartz. There are other driven wells at this station, 45 or 50 feet deep, which did not strike the ledge. At the South station, on Public street, there are also driven wells, one of them over 100 feet deep, which did not strike the ledge.

At the corner of Stewart and Conduit streets, about 70 feet above the sea, the ledge was struck at about 100 feet from the surface, mostly through sand.

On Field's Point, the ledge has not been struck at 60 feet depth. Test borings will probably be made there in connection with the proposed sewage works. The ledge was struck on Starve-goat Island, at 35 feet from the surface, and the well was carried to a depth of 129 feet, through rock, apparently like that at Silver Spring, East Providence.

At the works of the American Enamel Company, on the shore of Mashapaug Pond, the ledge was not struck at a depth of 200 feet, through sand and quick-sand.

At Moulter's What Cheer Brewery, Cranston, near Narragansett Park, the strata were 27 feet of gravel ; 208 feet of quick-sand ; 12 feet of ledge, Carboniferous, apparently like Fenner's ledge, making a total depth of 247 feet. The ledge was here reached at a depth of 235 feet, the deepest point at which Mr. Barker has known the ledge to be struck in this vicinity. He states that brewery sewage was drawn a distance of 125 feet into a well, through gravel.

At the Girls' Reform School, Sockanosset, Cranston, the drill went through 12 feet of tenacious marls, and struck a ledge of dark phyllite slate, followed by conglomerate, with much pyrite. An abundant supply of water was found at 156 feet depth.

At Saylesville, in the southern part of Lincoln, parties are now engaged in boring a deep artesian well. We understand that, at last accounts, it had reached the depth of 904 feet. The strata passed through, as far as we can learn, have been 10 feet of ordinary upper gravelly strata, 170 feet or more of fine bluish sand, 15 to 20 feet of coarse gravel, and 704 feet of solid rock. The rock seems to be a granite formation, at times wholly quartz.

Several wells, 50 to 70 feet deep, have been sunk on Warwick Neck, where the ledge is 12 to 15 feet below the surface, and apparently of graywacke, in some cases with pyrite cubes. The black Carboniferous shale is also found at Warwick Neck.

At River Point, a well has been sunk 82 feet, 22 feet of which was sand and gravel, and the remainder hard granite. In East Greenwich, the ledge was reached at 25 to 30 feet, — not coal measures. At Narragansett Pier, pink granite lies near the surface.

At Drownville, conglomerate rock was reached perhaps 12 feet from the surface, in a well of perhaps 50 feet depth. The Nayatt Brick Company sunk a well of 65 feet, through clay, reaching white gravel. A similar deposit of clay, reaching below 60 feet from the surface, is found in other parts of Barrington; also quick-sand and cobble-stones are found in the town.

At Bristol Neck, a well of about 90 feet passed through pink granite, lying near the surface. On the premises of the National Rubber Company, Bristol, is a well 625 feet deep. The ledge was struck a few feet below the surface. It is of granite, with occasional quartz and feldspar veins. The well does not yield water enough to pay for pumping.

At the Torpedo Station, Goat Island, Newport Harbor, a well was bored through "hard pan" to a ledge of light colored rock, rather soft, at 32 feet, reaching a depth of about 214 feet from the surface. On Coaster's Harbor Island, a well was sunk 87 feet, through black rock and conglomerate, obtaining a supply of excellent water. On Bath road, not far from Bellevue avenue, a well was sunk 112 feet, through variously colored rock, similar to those seen along the "Cliffs;" water poor.

VII. General Remarks.

The earlier parts of this Report have occupied much more space than was anticipated, and this concluding portion must, therefore, be made briefer than we had originally contemplated. Our chief purpose, however, has been to bring to the notice of the members of the Franklin Society what has already been learned about the Geology of Rhôde Island. An examination of the preceding pages will show what has been accomplished in that direction; and, by consulting the Index appended to this Report, information on any special topic can easily be obtained. We have attempted little original investigation, but have tried to lay the foundations essential to future progress.

The necessity for some such collation of authorities is apparent to one who seeks to gain a clear idea of the Geology of Rhode Island. Information is scattered through many publications, as the Index shows. Jackson's Report is incomplete and nearly obsolete, and there has been no later survey to collect information. The Franklin Society endeavored to secure a new survey of the State in 1875-6, and again made an effort for a topographical survey in 1885-6; but thus far nothing has been accomplished. This Report is published as the best contribution the Society can make to the cause, a step towards a complete survey; for a knowledge of what has already been learned is the proper foundation on which to build.

As early as 1820 to 1840 much attention was bestowed by members of the Franklin Society and others upon the minerals of Rhode Island; and when we consider the study that has since been given them, we conclude that the simple minerals of the State are now pretty well identified, with the exception of distinguishing the different species of feldspar, chlorite, etc. It is natural that minerals should be studied before rocks. Little has been done with the rocks of the State, and we have attempted no catalogue of them. There is need of a full study of the rocks of Rhode Island, such as is found in the New Hampshire report of Hawes, by means of microscopic sections and the modern methods for the separation of different minerals in rocks, and for chemical analysis, as outlined in Williams' "Modern Petrography," and the tenth volume of the tenth U. S. Census. Such a study a new geological survey should furnish.

The age of the rocks in Rhode Island has been but little studied since Jackson's time, with the exception, perhaps, of the Carboniferous area, the Lincoln limestones, and the southern portion of the State. The mouth of Narragansett Bay and the vicinity of Newport have been pretty fully studied by the Hitchcocks, Shaler, Hunt, Crosby, and Dale; and Dale's map of that region [p. 51 of this Report] is the most exact and complete of any yet published for any part of the State.

Various opinions have been entertained in regard to the age of the rocks of this State. The general tendency of the changes of opinion in later years has been to regard them as of later origin than was formerly supposed; but certain fluctuations, amounting almost to an ebb and flow of opinion, are noticeable. Different geologists have also, at nearly the same time, expressed widely different opinions. For instance, the rocks on Newport Neck called "chloritic argillyte" and "siliceous argillyte" by Dale, "flinty slate" by E. Hitchcock, and "metamorphic rocks" by Jackson, are made of Archean (Huronian) time by Hunt, Taconic or Shawmut group (that is pre-Potsdam or Cambrian) by Crosby, Primordial (lower Silurian or Ordovician) by Shaler, and possibly Silurian by Dale.

No one, so far as we know, with a single exception, has ever supposed any of the rocks of Rhode Island to be of Mesozoic age. That exception is the suggestion, arising no doubt from the color, that the red rock of Central Falls might be Triassic; but this rock is now regarded as Carboniferous. The range of opinion then is, Paleozoic, Archean, or igneous.

One class of rocks may now be considered as settled in age,

and furnishing a standard with which to compare the others. These are the rocks of the region about Narragansett Bay, running north-easterly into Massachusetts, now considered of Carboniferous age. Maclure, in 1809, called the anthracite bearing strata of both Rhode Island and Pennsylvania " Transition." Cleaveland, in 1816, used the same term for the Rhode Island area. Jackson, in 1840; used the term " Transition Grau-wacke." He stated that, " from the fossils alone," a geologist would make the grau-wacke rocks of Rhode Island " identical with the bituminous coal measures of England ;" but the order of superposition, and the structure and composition of the rocks themselves led him to consider the Rhode Island rocks more ancient. In 1840, E. Hitchcock first suggested that a portion of this area, previously considered more ancient, might be of Carboniferous age,—a position approved by Johnson, Lyell, and others, but opposed by Emmons,—and in 1853 he advanced a step further, declared the whole tract Carboniferous, the Rhode Island coal of the same age as the other coal of the United States and of Europe, and gave his reasons therefor. In 1860, C. H. Hitchcock advocated the same view, and it has been generally adopted since that time.

In 1880, the Carboniferous area was still further extended by Crosby and Barton, who added to it the red and green slates, sandstones and conglomerates of Central Falls and Cumberland, previously referred, doubtfully, to the Devonian or Old Red Sandstone, by E. Hitchcock, Lyell, and Crosby. Crosby and Barton conclude that the lowest or conglomerate rocks of the Central Falls series are older than the true coal measures, and are the equivalent of the Millstone Grit ; and that there is no true Sub-Carboniferous in Massachusetts or Rhode Island.

The other rocks of the State, excepting, of course, Tertiary and more recent deposits, underlie the Carboniferous, and are more ancient. This class includes the greater portion of the rocks of the State. None of them have been certainly decided to be of Silurian or Devonian age, though Shaler and Dale suggest that some rocks in Newport and vicinity may be Silurian, and the Lingulæ pebbles of the Carboniferous conglomerate were probably derived from lower Silurian rocks.

These ancient rocks were called "Primitive" by Cleaveland, and "Primary" by Jackson, who considered most of them to be of igneous origin. The "hornblende rock" of Cumberland, Lincoln, and Johnston, he regarded as igneous, also, though sometimes appearing to be stratified.* The limestone contained in it, although stratified, presents no fossils; hence we are left in doubt whether it was the result of life, with the fossils obliterated by metamorphism, or was formed by chemical deposition, according to the theory of Hunt. The same crystalline structure and absence of fossils characterize the whole "Primary" and "hornblende" formation in Rhode Island, and render the age uncertain.

Dana marks these crystalline rocks of Rhode Island as undetermined,—that is, they may be Archean, Silurian, or Devonian. Most recent geologists consider the greater part of them, at least, Archean, a term which includes both Azoic and Eozoic. The maps of C. H. Hitchcock, 1874–1886, differ from each other, and some of them give Silurian in the northern parts of the State; but in all of them he gives most of the territory under consideration as Archean (Laurentian, Huronian, and Montalban), and in the last one it is wholly Archean (Laurentian), with no Silurian. The map of the U. S. Geological Survey published in 1884 gives this area as Archean. Crosby calls most of the crystalline rocks of Rhode Island Archean (either Montalban or Huronian), including the hornblende rock and limestones before mentioned;† but Emmons called the limestones Taconic, and Shaler has recently suggested that they are probably Sub-Carboniferous. Dale has also recently said ‡ that it would not be surprising if some metamorphic rocks, now regarded as of Archean age, "should be ultimately found to belong to the Paleozoic."

---

*Pp. 18, 19, 30, 31, Jackson, and pp. 9, 10, this Report.
†Pp. 41, 42 of this Report.
‡P. 52 of this Report.

Enough has been stated to indicate the difficulty of determining the age of these crystalline rocks of Rhode Island, and the necessity for further study of these rocks, which occupy so large a part of the State.

The surface geology of Rhode Island offers a rich field for investigation. Dana has published a paper which treats of the shores of Narragansett Bay, Shaler one of Newport, and Upham and Chamberlin have given us the results of their study of the glacial terminal moraines in the southern part of the State;* but, with these exceptions, little has been done, and in the greater part of the State glacial effects, drift, etc., have not been studied at all. We hope to see this department as fully presented in a new survey of Rhode Island as was done in the last New Hampshire survey.

As a basis for all this geological work, and especially for that last mentioned, exact topographical maps are essential. When describing the Massachusetts maps, *Science* well says: "Enough has been done in the broad, vague way of distant continental homologies: what is now needed is the local examination of minute topographic details, so that we may learn to see and appreciate the forms about us at home; and nothing will lead sooner or surer to this long-delayed end than the publication of good topographic maps. The educational value of these maps will alone repay the people of Massachusetts over and over again for their share in the cost of making them."

The following references could not be inserted in their proper order in Part I., and are therefore printed here.

1804. *New York Medical Repository.* "Disclosures in Mineralogy: from specimens brought to Dr. Mitchell." Green Serpentine from Newport, R. I. Dark green, with spots of paler green, "verging in some parts toward a yellow or whitish;" smooths and polishes well, possesses a fine grain;

---

* P. 25, 26, 31, 32, 37-39, 46, 47 of this Report.

"an handsome serpentine, and apparently well worthy of being worked."

1844. EBENEZER EMMONS. "The Taconic System, based on observations in N. Y., Mass., Me., Vt., and R. I.," 68 pp. and 6 plates. Same as "Agriculture," below, so far as R. I. is concerned.

1846. EBENEZER EMMONS. "Natural History of New York, Part V., Agriculture," Vol. 1. Allusions to the R. I. coal beds and "Old Red Sandstone," pp. 53–55, 76. Arguments against the doctrine of Lyell and others that the R. I. anthracite is a metamorphic coal, with the bitumen dissipated by heat; veins of quartz not injected in a state of igneous fusion, but "deposited from a vapor or water holding silex in solution."

"The Taconic System in Rhode Island," pp. 90–93. The Smithfield limestone is clearly stratified, but from its intimate relation to igneous rocks "has undergone a change in texture," and the peculiar minerals saussurite and nephrite have been developed, with talc in greater quantities than in any beds of limestone examined by Emmons elsewhere. It is of the age of the Stockbridge limestone (Berkshire marble) of the Taconic system, and "differs from the Primary limestone of St. Lawrence and Essex counties, New York, in being stratified, and in the absence of graphite, spinelle," etc. He finds other members of the Taconic system in the adjacent magnesian slate containing serpentine and epidote, quartz rock, etc.; and gives a section (Fig. 13) exhibiting "the relation of the Taconic rocks of Smithfield and Cumberland, together with the adjacent rocks upon the west and east," containing a trap dyke or thin bed of hornblende in the limestone. Only a fragment of the system remains, vast portions having been worn away by denuding agents, and carried into other systems, giving yellow soils, beds of hematite, etc.

1854. LEO LESQUEREUX. *Boston Journal of Natural History*, vol. 6, pp. 409–431. "New Species of Fossil Plants,

from the Anthracite and Bituminous Coal-fields of Penn."
Descriptions, without plates, with introduction by H. D.
Rogers. All these are undoubtedly included in the later works
of Lesquereux. Reports on Ill., Penn., etc.

1881. G. W. Hawes, C. Kelly, G. P. Merrill, and
N. S. Shaler. *Tenth Census of the United States*, Vol. X.
" Report on the Building Stones of the United States and Statistics of the Quarry Industry for 1880." Description of
Westerly "biotite granite," p. 20, plate xxxix [Merrill],
quoted p. 92 of this Report.

Statistics of "crystalline siliceous rocks" quarried in R. I.,
capital invested, amount and value of product, etc., of 17
quarries collectively, tables I, II, III, pp. 46–51.

Location, quarry owners, variety of stone, color, structure,
and geological age of each of the 17 quarries reported in R. I.,
Table IV., pp. 56, 57. Eight of these are in Westerly (including 1 at Niantic), 3 in W. Greenwich, and 1 each at
Newport, Cranston, Smithfield* (4 miles E. of), Diamond Hill,
Woonsocket, and Pascoag. Thirteen yield biotite granite, 2
gneissoid granite (Pascoag biotite gneiss, and Diamond Hill
hornblende gneiss) and 2 mica-schist (Cranston Fenner and
Woonsocket). All are given as of Archean age except the
Cranston Fenner ledge (Carboniferous?). Other quarries of
the State are not included, either because no reports were received, or because less than $1,000 worth of stone was quarried in the year 1880.

Shaler's brief report on the building stones of R. I. Limestone N. and E. of Providence "probably belonging to the
Lower Coal Measures or the sub-Carboniferous limestone," p.
107. "Syenites"† of Westerly and Bristol; limestones too

---

* Quarry in the south-eastern part of Smithfield, near the North Providence line. The Smithfield Granite Company also has another quarry in Johnston, about one mile west of Snake Den, called the Wm. Waterman quarry. The Thurber quarry, which has not been worked for a number of years, lies between Snake Den and Bear Rock.

† We fail to see how the term "syenite" applies, either according to the definition of Hawes, or the different one of Dana.

much rent by joints for building stones;* conglomerates of the Coal Measures fitted for architectural purposes, p. 110.

Stone Construction in Newport, p. 312; Pawtucket, pp. 337-8; Providence,† pp. 349, 350; Woonsocket, pp. 362-3. This gives the character and source of stone used in various buildings. Stone from the Nipmuck ledge, near Coventry, is here mentioned as used in Providence, though not included in the preceding tables.

1886. RAPHAEL PUMPELLY. *Tenth Census of the U. S.*, 1880, Vol. XV. Analysis of magnetic iron ore from Iron Mine Hill, Cumberland, pp. 566-7. Coal of the Mass.-R. I. area [F. Prime, Jr.], p. 605. Statistics concerning production of R. I. coal in 1880, pp. 625-630.

1886. CHARLES D. WALCOTT. *Bulletin of the U. S. Geolog. Survey*, vol. iv, No. 30. "Second Contribution to the Studies of the Cambrian Faunas of North America." Notice in *Science*, vol. ix, No. 226, pp. 545-6. Divides early Paleozoic (omitting the supposed pre-Cambrian) into Cambrian, Ordovician (lower Silurian), and Silurian (upper Silurian). Confirms Emmons' work on the Taconic system; central idea of Emmons "now known to be correct," "in classifying the Upper Taconic as pre-Potsdam." Walcott uses Cambrian in place of Taconic.

1887. J. W. DAWSON. *Science*, vol. 9, p. 590. Uses terms Cambrian and Ordovician (Siluro-Cambrian), as above.

1887. *Providence Journal.* "Our own Coal and Iron." Letter of W. F. Durfee on R. I. iron and coal, June 3.

"The Cranston Mines. Rhode Island Coal an Important Factor in the State's Commerce." After remaining comparatively idle for 12 years, the mine is now worked, in a new

---

* Harris limestone was used for trimmings in building Hope College, Brown University, in 1822.

† Various inaccuracies are noted in the portion relating to Providence, as may be seen by comparing with R. I. Census of 1885. The Arcade columns and the First Congregational church are said to be of "Smithfield granite"; Saint Stephen's church, of Conn. brownstone (probably Grace church is meant); "Sayles Memorial church at Brown's university," etc.

shaft, by the N. Y. Carbon Iron Co., and the coal shipped to Pittsburgh, to be used in making wrought iron. Feasibility of profitably manufacturing pig iron from Cumberland ore, mixed with foreign ores, with the use of R. I. coal. Gas wells possible in R. I. June 7.

" Coal and Iron. Rhode Island Products and how they can be used." Report of addresses of W. F. Durfee, ex-Gov. Lippitt, and others, before the Board of Trade; proposal to start blast furnaces at tide water; quotations from various authorities on the value of R. I. coal and iron, with R. I. limestone for flux. June 8.

" The Cranston Mines. — A Curiosity." Quality of Cranston coal; remarkable spring near the mines. June 8.

" Hon. James S. Negley on R. I. Coal and Iron." Extract from *N. Y. Tribune*. June 10.

"A New Artesian Well in Fall River." Strata passed through, Carboniferous formation. July 16.

" Rhode Island Coal," iron ore, and fire clays, July 23, from *Springfield Republican*. Shaler's discussion in report of U. S. Geol. Survey;* says Cranston coal is shipped to Pittsburgh to be used in making steel.

" Rhode Island's Mineral Wealth," July 30, " Geological Surveys," Aug. 1, " The Need of a Geological Survey of the State," Aug. 2, three editorial articles; also " Rhode Island Affairs in Washington," Aug. 2, correspondence, Geol. Survey* on the State's Mineral Springs (6 localities and 17 springs), and Prof. Shaler's plan for the reclamation of marshes (list of marshes with number of acres in each).

1887. HENRY GANNETT. *Science*, July 29, vol. x, pp. 49–53. " Topographical Survey of the United States." Full details, with cost, etc.

In the previous number of *Science*, p. 37, is an editorial paragraph on " The Demand from Railway Corporations for the Geological Survey Maps."

---

*A brief statement, giving a synopsis of work done, appears in the Sixth Annual Report of the Director, for 1884-5. The full report on the Narragansett field awaits the completion of the topographic maps, and it may be some years before it appears.

1886–7. T. NELSON DALE. *Proc. Newport Nat. Hist. Soc.*, Document 5. " List of Minerals and Rocks occurring in the vicinity of Newport." [Not yet published].

1887. AMOS PERRY. R. I. State Census of 1885. Interesting localities, sources of stones for various buildings, etc. [Advance sheets, only, yet printed].

About 1885. M. E. WADSWORTH. " Descriptive Catalogue of One Hundred Thin Sections of American and Foreign Rocks, for the use of Students of Microscopical Lithology." Boston : The Prang Educational Co. Sections 1 and 2, p. 5, are " Pallasite, var. Cumberlandite", from Iron Mine Hill, Cumberland. R. I. No. 1 is titaniferous magnetite, with crystals of olivine and plagioclase ; No. 2 is the altered rock, containing serpentine and actinolite, without feldspar. Refers to Proc. Boston Soc. Nat. Hist., 1881, xxi, 195–197. See also p. 44 of this Report.

Rev. Edgar F. Clark has recently found some interesting fossils, at Division street, Pawtucket, which have not yet been fully identified. One of them somewhat resembles a trilobite; but a close inspection shows that it does not belong to that family, although it is an articulate. In a letter just received, Prof. Scudder says : " The fossil which you sent from the Pawtucket coal is a fragment of an *Anthracomartus*, a carboniferous genus of Arachnida, and is possibly new. I have described two species from this country, and it appears to be distinct from them, but whether it is distinct from all of the species of the European coal beds I could not undertake to say without giving it a closer study than I have now time for. . . . The two published American species, *A. trilobitus* and *A. pustulatus*, came, the first from Arkansas, the second from Illinois."

DAVID W. HOYT.
WELCOME O. BROWN,
CHARLES M. SALISBURY, } *Committee.*
THOMAS J. BATTEY,
THOMAS H. SHURROCKS,

PROVIDENCE, September, 1887.

INDEX.

Absence of fossils, 108.
Absence of sand, 26.
Academy. (See Connecticut, Journal, Proceedings.)
Actinolite, 7, 67, 83, 84, 90, 93, 114.
Adams, 5, 14.
Address on R. I. coal mines, 6.
Adhémar, 45, 47.
Adirondacks, 20, 24.
Agassiz, 8, 12, 13, 27.
Agate, 66, 83.
Age of R. I. coal, 12, 14, 16, 19, 20, 107, 110.
Age of R. I. rocks, 106-109.
Aldrich, 60.
Alethopteris, 68, 69, 72, 74.
Alger, 14.
Alkalies, removal of, 20.
Alleghanies, 30.
Allen, 33.
Alluvial formation, 3, 13.
Alluvium, 19, 64.
Almy, 58.
Almy Farm, 90.
Aluminous rocks, 20.
American Assoc. Adv. Science, 18, 24, 44. (See Proceedings.)
American Enamel Co., 103.
American Geog. Soc., 32.
American Inst. Min. Eng. (See Transactions.)
American Journal of Science, 4-8, 10, 12, 14-16, 18, 20, 21, 24, 25, 27, 31, 32, 35-37, 41, 43, 44, 47, 49-51, 54, 79.
American Mineralog. Journal, 3.
American Naturalist, 24, 25, 27, 28, 36, 39, 53, 68, 72.
American Phil. Soc., 3, 5.
American Soc. Civ. Eng., 55.
Amethyst, 5, 6, 11, 56, 82, 92.
Amianthus, 84.
Amphibole, 84.
Amphibolic aggregate, 11, 57.
Amygdaloid, 24.
Analysis, chemical, 106.
Analysis of Bowenite, 4.
Analysis of Coal, 3, 6, 23, 34, 54, 86, 87, 90, 93.
Analysis of Iron ore, 34, 87, 112.
Analysis of Knebelite, 87.

Analysis of Limestone, 62, 87, 88, 90, 94, 95.
Analysis of Masonite, 14, 15, 91.
Analysis of Nephrite, 4.
Analysis of Soils, 9.
Andover, 43.
Augell, 61.
Angular stones, 97.
Annularia, 48, 51, 69, 76.
Annals Lyc. Nat. Hist., 5, 7.
Anthony, 6.
Anthracite, 3, 4, 6, 7, 12, 14, 17, 19, 23, 28, 34, 41, 52, 63, 64, 86, 87, 90, 91, 93, 94, 107, 110, 111. (See Coal.)
Anthracomartus, 114.
Anticlinal, 11, 42.
Apatite, 20, 31, 52, 81, 87, 92.
Aphlebia, 75.
Appalachian, 20, 24, 36.
Apponaug, 5, 91.
Aquidneck Island, 16, 18, 19, 25-27, 48, 50, 51.
Aquidneck Coal Co., 3.
Aquidneck mine, 16.
Arachnida, 114.
Arcade columns, 90, 112.
Archæopteris, 75.
Archean, 2, 29, 31, 51, 52, 55-57, 106-109, 111.
Area R. I. and Mass. coal measures, 21.
Argentiferous galena, 65.
Argentine limestone, 62, 82.
Argillaceous iron ore, 65.
Argillaceous schist, 51.
Argillite, 7, 20, 26, 42, 51, 52.
Arnold, 62, 67.
Arnold's quarry, 88.
Arsenopyrite, 80, 87.
Artesian wells, 57, 81, 95, 97-105, 113.
Articulate, 114. (See Insect.)
Arvonian, 53.
Asbestus, 4, 52, 64, 66, 67, 83, 84, 91, 96.
Ashton, 80.
Asphalt pavement, 88.
Association Amer. Geol., 12, 13.
Asterophyllites, 49, 69, 76, 77.
Atco, 45.
Atlantic formation, 29.

Atmospheric changes, 20, 89.
Attleboro', 14, 63.
Augite, 84.
Austin's Point, 58.
Azoic, 2, 36, 52, 53, 108.
Azurite, 80.

Babbitt, 6.
Babel, 83.
Backbone of L. I., 13.
Baker, 6.
Balanced rocks, 94. (See Rocking stones.)
Ballou, 2, 60.
Baltimorite, 86.
Barber's Height, 50.
Barbour, 15.
Barker, 95, 98, 100, 102-105.
Barrington, 104.
Barstow Stove Co., 102.
Barton, 43, 56, 107.
Basalt, 6.
Basanite, 83.
Battey, 56, 114.
Beacon Hill, 34, 35.
Beacon Pole Hill, 59, 87.
Bear Rock, 90, 111.
Beaver Tail, 51.
Bed-rock. (See Ledge.)
Belgium, 16.
Bennett's, 65.
Bergeria, 77.
Berkeley's Seat, 51.
Berkshire marble, 110.
Beryl, 84, 92.
Biotite, 44, 85, 92, 94, 111.
Bishop's Rock, 50.
Bitter spar, 82.
Bitumen dissipated, 110.
Black sand, 98. (See Iron sand.)
Blackstone River, 41, 81, 82.
Black Point, 48.
Blake, 22, 28, 29, 63.
Blatta, 49.
Blende, 65.
Block Island, 2, 5, 9, 13, 14, 32-35, 37-39, 41, 45, 53, 56, 65, 66, 80, 81, 84-86, 94.
Blue asbestus, 84.
Board of Trade, 113.
Bog iron ore, 23, 65, 81, 94.
Bonnet Point, 50.
Boring. (See Digging, Artesian.)
Bornia, 76.
Bornite, 80.
Boston, 3, 4, 6, 15, 21, 23, 28, 30, 31, 37, 45, 55, 57, 58, 114.
Boston basin, 30, 42, 43.
Boston Journ. Nat. Hist., 14, 69, 110.
Boston Neck, 58.
Boston Soc. Nat. Hist. (See Memoirs, Proceedings.)

Botryoidal chalcedony, 83.
Botryoidal hematite, 65, 80.
Boulders, 5, 10-13, 19, 26-28, 30, 31 33, 34, 38, 45, 47, 48, 52, 54, 56, 64, 81, 87-92, 94, 95, 97-99.
Bourn, 55.
Bowen, 4.
Bowenite, 4, 15, 67, 86, 88.
Bowlders. (See Boulders.)
Braintree, 42, 43.
Brande's Iron Works, 58, 60.
Breccia, 62.
Brewery sewage, 103.
Bristol, 5, 6, 11, 12, 49, 53, 63, 64, 66, 73, 76-80, 82-84, 86, 92, 93, 104, 111.
Bristol County, 15, 16, 42.
Bristol Ferry, 92.
Bristol Neck, 64, 67, 92, 104.
Broad Hills, 38.
Brongniart, 68-78.
Brown, 56, 62, 65, 114.
Brown and Sharpe Co., 101.
Brown hematite, 65, 81.
Brown spar, 7, 66, 82.
Brown's quarry, 59, 62, 67, 68, 90.
Brown University, 71, 73, 74, 76, 88, 112.
Bruce, 3.
Brush, 8, 15.
Buffalo, 55.
Building stones, 111, 112, 114.
Bulletin Museum Comp. Zoöl., 44, 52.
Bulletin U. S. Geol. Surv., 53, 112.
Bunbury, 69, 71.
Bunker Hill, 38.
Burleigh, 53.
Burbank, 33.
Burrillville, 11, 56, 60, 82, 83, 86, 95.
Butterfly factory, 88.

Cacholong, 67, 83.
Calamariæ, 75-77.
Calamites, 64, 69, 75, 76, 91.
Calamostachys, 49, 77.
Calciferous mica slate, 60.
Calcite, 61, 62, 81, 85, 88. (See Limestone.)
Calc-spar, 61, 81.
Callipteridium, 72.
Calumet Hill, 53, 80, 87.
Cambrian, 10, 24, 30, 36, 43, 45, 79, 106, 112.
Cambrian faunas, 112.
Cambridge, 30, 44, 52.
Canada, 14, 21, 22, 36, 52, 56.
Canadian Naturalist, 24, 28.
Canadian Geol. Survey, 21, 53.
Cannon cast, 34.
Cape Cod, 23, 26, 28, 34, 37, 39, 44, 45.
Carbonaceous slate, 64, 67, 96.
Carbonates, formation of, 20.

INDEX. 117

Carbonic acid in air, 20.
Carboniferous flora, 40, 41, 53, 68-79.
Carboniferous formation, 2-4, 6-12, 14-24, 26-31, 34, 40-43, 50-57, 62-64, 68-79, 93, 94, 96, 98-104, 106-108, 110-113.
Carbon Iron Co., 113.
Carnelian, 8, 83.
Case's mine, 16, 63.
Castle Hill, 82, 86.
Catalogue, Jackson's, 58-68.
Catalogue of fossils, 68-79.
Catalogue of geol. maps, 53.
Catalogue of geol. surveys, 40. (See Reports.)
Catalogues of minerals, 6, 8, 65-68, 79-86, 114.
Cat's eye, 82.
Census, R. I., 112, 114.
Census, U. S., 92, 106, 111, 112.
Center of gravity of earth, 45, 47.
Central Falls, 43, 81, 83, 106, 107.
Chace, 33.
Chalcedony, 66, 83.
Chalcopyrite. (See Copper pyrites.)
Chamberlin, 46, 47, 49, 109.
Champlain Island, 29.
Champlain period, 26-28, 31, 32, 36, 49.
Changes of level, 29, 42. (See Land.)
Changes of opinion, 106.
Channing, 33.
Charles River, 23.
Charlestown, 38, 92.
Charts, coast survey, 27, 33, 41.
Chasms, 31, 50, 93. (See Fissures.)
Chemical. (See Analysis.)
Chemical deposition of rocks, 108. (See Hunt.)
Chert, 19.
Chesterlite, 85.
Chin Hill, 38.
Chlorite, 8, 19, 51, 52, 68, 83, 86, 87, 90, 93, 94, 106.
Chlorite-spar, 15.
Chloritic argillyte, 51, 106.
Chloritic rock, 68.
Chloritic schist, 20, 51.
Chloritic slate, 42, 61, 62.
Chloritoid, 15, 86.
Chlorophane, 81.
Church, 64.
Church's quarry, 62.
Chrysolite, 44, 84, 94.
Chrysolitic iron ore, 81.
Chrysotile, 86.
Citrine, 82.
City engineer, 40, 95, 99, 101.
Claremont, 21.

Clark, 49, 55, 69-79, 114.
Clay, 28, 31, 33-35, 38, 39, 50, 52, 54, 64, 94, 97-104.
Clay Head, 35, 38.
Clay iron stone, 80, 94.
Clay slate, 52.
Clayville, 59.
Cleaveland, 3, 107, 108.
Cliffs, 50, 105.
Coal, 2-4, 6-8, 10, 12, 14-17, 19, 22-24, 28, 34, 41, 47, 52, 54, 55, 63, 64, 86, 87, 90, 91, 93, 94, 96, 98, 107, 110-112, 113. (See Age, Analysis.)
Coal ashes, 63, 64.
Coal companies, 2, 3, 8, 23, 113.
Coal fields, 15, 16, 19, 20, 22, 28, 52, 69, 110, 111.
Coal flora, 40, 41, 53, 68-79.
Coal measures, 2, 11, 16, 17, 19, 26-28, 29, 43, 49, 51, 52, 62-64, 69, 104, 107, 110-112. (See Area.)
Coal mines, 3, 6, 15, 16, 19, 23, 41, 62, 64, 65, 87, 91, 93, 112, 113.
Coal, statistics of, 17, 112.
Coaster's Harbor Island, 19, 50, 105.
Coast Survey, 25-27, 33, 41.
Cobble-stones, 54, 102, 104.
Coddington Cove, 50.
College Hill, 90.
Coloration of geol. maps, 56.
Commission of 1876, 9, 33.
Committee, appointment, 1; names, 114.
Conanicut Island, 10, 50-52, 61, 86, 94. (See Jamestown.)
Concord, 14, 29.
Concretion, 92.
Conglomerate, 6, 10-12, 16, 18-22, 26, 27, 29-31, 33, 42, 43, 48, 49, 51, 52, 63, 88, 91-93, 96, 101, 103-105, 107, 108, 112.
Conglomerate, formation of, 52.
Congress, Geological, 56.
Connecticut, 8, 12, 13, 34, 41.
Connecticut Academy of Arts and Sciences, 7, 27.
Connecticut Geol. Reports, 8, 12, 13.
Connecticut River, 13, 15, 25, 32, 47, 49.
Connecticut valley, 17, 25, 36, 44.
Contents of this Report, 1.
Cook, 36, 48, 58, 60.
Copperas, 66, 81.
Copper carbonate, 65, 80.
Copper mine, 65.
Copper Mine Hill, 87.
Copper ore, 10, 11, 87.
Copper pyrites, 65, 66, 80.
Coral, 35.

Cordaiteæ, 78.
Cordaites, 78.
Cost of topog. surveys, 113.
Cove basin, 57, 101, 102.
Coventry, 82, 84-86, 94, 112.
Cranberry Hill, 38.
Cranston, 16, 19, 23, 34, 54, 59, 61-65, 67, 80-86, 91, 100, 102, 103, 111.
Cranston coal mine, 34, 54, 91, 112, 113.
Cranston iron mine, 23, 34, 59, 65, 67, 80, 91.
Crenitic theory, 57.
Cretaceous, 28, 50.
Crocidolite, 84.
Croll, 47.
Crosby, 36, 41-43, 50, 56, 79, 106-108.
Crystalline rocks, 2, 20, 23, 24, 30, 36, 45, 52, 57-59, 108, 109, 111. (See Origin.)
Crystallography, 35.
Cumberland, 2-7, 9-12, 16, 19, 23, 41, 43-45, 53, 58-68, 79-87, 107, 108, 110, 112, 114.
Cumberland coal mine, 62, 64, 65, 87.
Cumberland Hill, 58-62, 65-68, 87.
Cumberland iron boulders, 10, 12, 19, 64, 81.
Cumberland iron ore, 10, 23, 34, 44, 45, 53, 55, 57, 60, 65-67, 81, 85, 87, 112-114.
Cumberlandite, 114.
Cuttyhunk, 33.
Cyanite, 4, 85.
Cyclopteris, 71.

Dale, 48, 50-52, 57, 61, 81, 85, 86, 93, 94, 106, 108, 114.
Damming of streams, 32, 46.
Dana, E. S., 8, 35.
Dana, J. D., 8, 14, 21, 25, 27, 28, 31, 32, 44, 47, 49, 79, 108, 109, 111.
Date of glacial era, 41, 43, 44.
Davis, 6, 45, 46, 54.
Dawson, 112.
De la Beche, 13.
Demand for maps, 113.
Dendrites, 62, 82, 83, 88.
Dendritic talc, 86.
Denison, 40.
Devil's Foot, 60, 94.
Devonian, 14, 16, 24, 26, 43, 107, 108.
Dexter. (See Lime Rock.)
Diamond Hill, 59, 66, 67, 80-83, 87, 111.
Diamond Hill quarry, 87.
Dictyopteris, 68, 69, 71.
Digging and Boring, 95-105.
Dighton, 19.
Dikes. (See Dykes.)
Diluvial currents, 12.

Diluvial grooves, 10.
Diluvium, 64.
Diorite, 20, 24.
Dip, 11, 16, 19, 23, 41, 48, 50, 89, 96.
Direction. (See Glacial motion, Gla. striae, Transportation.)
Disintegrating rock, 89.
Distortion of pebbles, 11, 18, 19, 21, 22, 27, 29, 31, 33, 42, 93.
Distortion theories, 18, 19, 21, 22, 31, 93.
Division line between till and modified drift, 96, 97.
Dodge, 30.
Dog-tooth spar, 82.
Dolomite, 11, 12, 19, 20, 23, 24, 29, 42, 82, 87, 88. (See Magnesian, Origin.)
Double-refraction spar, 82.
Drift, 2, 11, 13, 19, 23, 26, 28, 29, 32, 34-39, 45-47, 54, 97, 109. (See Boulders, Clay, Cobble-stones, Gravel, Hills, Pebbles, Sand, Till, Transportation.)
Drift, depressions in. (See Glacial depressions.)
Drift direction, 13. (See Glacial striae, Transportation.)
Drift-hills, 54. (See Hills.)
Drift, modified, 29, 31, 38, 39, 90, 97, 100.
Drift sections, 45.
Drift, theories of, 13. (See Glacial, Iceberg.)
Drift, unmodified, 97. (See Till, Hard-pan.)
Drownville, 104.
Drumlins, 45, 54.
Drum Rock, 5, 91.
Drums, 54.
Dumplings, 19, 52, 85, 94.
Dunes, 36.
Durfee, 112, 113.
Durfee's ledge, 64, 91.
Dutch Island, 50, 51.
Dyerville, 100.
Dykes, 10, 31, 36, 56, 59, 93, 110.

Eagle Park, 100.
Earth's center of gravity, 45, 47.
East Greenwich, 32, 82-84, 104.
East Haven, 13.
East Island, 51.
Easton, 18.
Easton's Beach, 50.
Easton's Point, 19, 48, 51.
East Providence, 78, 79, 81, 84, 86, 91, 99, 103.
Eaton, 4, 7.
Eddy, 5, 53.
Edinboro', 17.
Edward's, 60, 67.

Elizabeth Islands, 33, 34, 37, 39.
Elliptical hills, 54.
Elm Farm, 80, 90.
Elongation of pebbles. (See Distortion.)
Emmons, A. B., 54.
Emmons, E., 17, 85, 107, 108, 110, 112.
Engineer and Mining Journal, 57.
England, 16, 107.
Eozoan, 52.
Eozoic, 2, 28, 29, 52, 108.
Epidote, 7, 61, 67, 85, 87, 92, 94, 110.
Epidote rock, 20, 59.
Eremopteris, 70.
Erosion, 13, 15, 17, 22, 25, 30, 31, 47. (See Glacial, Excavation.)
Eruptive rocks, 37, 44, 51, 57. (See Igneous.)
Eskers, 34, 41.
Essays, Chem. and Geol., 21, 28.
Essex Co., N. Y., 110.
Estuary formations, 31.
Europe, 7, 16, 27.
Excavation of lake basins, 22, 31, 45, 46.
Exeter, 91.

Faces, natural, 88, 91.
Fall River, 10, 18, 31, 43, 79, 113.
Fall River News, 57.
False topaz, 82.
Farmington, 49.
Fasiculite, 84.
Faults, 11, 30, 49.
Faunas, 79, 112, 114.
Feldspar, 11, 20, 24, 44, 58, 67, 85, 87, 92-94, 104, 106, 114.
Feldspar rock, 59.
Felsite, 26, 42.
Fenner's ledge, 91, 102, 103, 111.
Ferns, fossil, 64, 68-75.
Ferns, fossil, no. of. 79.
Ferruginous. (See Iron.)
Ferruginous conglomerate, 101.
Field's Point, 90, 103.
Filicaceæ, 68-75.
Fiords, 25, 28, 36.
Fire-clays, 113.
Firestone, 61, 65.
First Cong. Ch., 89, 112.
Fisher's Island, 13, 37, 39.
Fissures, 48, 49, 50, 93. (See Chasm, Joints.)
Flinty slate, 11, 42, 51, 61, 81.
Floating island, 88.
Floods, 31, 32, 47, 56, 97.
Floras, 40, 41, 53, 68-79.
Fluorite. (See Fluor-spar.)
Fluor-spar, 4, 5, 66, 81, 86, 87, 90, 92.
Flux, 113.
Folds, 30, 32, 49. (See Anticlinal.)

Fort Adams, 8, 10, 61-63, 94.
Fort Hill, 38.
Fortification agate, 83.
Fossil animals, 43, 49, 55, 79, 114. (See Lingula.)
Fossil fruits, 56, 78.
Fossil plants, 4, 14, 16, 19, 48, 49, 53, 56, 64, 68-79, 87, 90-94, 110.
Fossils, 4, 12, 14, 16-19, 26, 31, 32, 38, 40, 41, 43, 48, 49, 51, 53, 55, 56, 64, 68-79, 87, 90-94, 108, 110, 112, 114.
Fossils, absence of, 108.
Fossils, catalogue of, 68-79.
Fossils obliterated, 108.
Foster, 5, 13, 65, 80-82, 84-86.
Foster Banking Co., 65.
Fox Point, 99.
France, 16.
Franklin Society, 1, 6, 33, 53, 55, 56, 58, 61, 68, 105.
French chalk, 86.
Furnaces, iron, 55, 57, 113.
Fusion of anthracite, 4.

Galena, 65, 80, 87.
Galenite. (See Galena.)
Gannett, 113.
Gardiner's Island, 38.
Gardner, 32.
Garnet, 52, 67, 84, 86, 87, 92, 94.
Gasholder, 103.
Gas, natural, 57, 113.
Gay Head, 37, 38.
Geinitz, 69, 72, 76, 78.
General Assembly, 2, 3, 8, 9, 22, 33, 55, 57.
General Remarks, 105-106.
Geneva, 100.
Geodes, 81, 83.
Geological Congress, 56.
Geological Magazine, 57.
Geological Railway Guide, 40.
Geological. (See Journal, Maps, Reports, Sections, Surveys.)
Geology, general works on, 3, 4, 17, 21.
Germar, 69, 76.
Gibbs, 48.
Girls' Reform School, 103.
Glacial deposits, 23, 26, 34, 38, 39, 45, 50. (See Drift, Drumlins, Eskers, Kames, Moraines, etc.)
Glacial depressions, 13, 25, 33, 34, 45, 46.
Glacial erosion, 22, 26, 30, 31, 45-47, 51.
Glacial floods, 31, 32, 47, 49.
Glacial motion, 25, 27, 31, 44, 46, 49, 54, 94. (See Transportation.)
Glacial period, 2, 22, 23, 25-31, 37, 40, 41, 43-47, 49. (See Date.)

120 GEOLOGY OF RHODE ISLAND.

Glacial periods, several, 26, 27, 30, 31, 45, 46, 49.
Glacial streams, 25, 48.
Glacial striae, 10, 11, 13, 19, 25–27, 30, 38–40, 45, 47, 54, 87, 89–94.
Glacial theories, 8, 12, 13, 27, 29, 44–47, 52, 54.
Glaciated area of N. Amer., 53.
Glacier, head of New Eng., 25.
Glacier, melting of, 31.
Glaciers and their effects, 2, 8, 12, 13, 17, 22, 23, 25–41, 43–54, 56, 89–94, 97, 109. (See Fiords, Transportation.)
Glaciers, continental, 26, 28, 31, 45.
Glaciers, local, 27, 28.
Glocester, 81, 82, 85, 95.
Gneiss, 9, 10, 13, 17, 20, 21, 28, 33, 37, 41, 51, 59, 60, 85, 87, 89, 92, 94, 111.
Goat Island, 50, 104.
Goeppert, 69, 71, 72, 74, 78.
Gold, 80, 95.
Goniopteris, 73, 74.
Gooch, 54.
Governors' messages, 33, 55, 57.
Grace Church, 112.
Granite, 9–13, 17, 19, 24, 34, 41, 42, 50, 51, 58, 60, 62, 67, 85, 87–92, 94, 103, 104, 111, 112.
Grant, 58.
Graphite, 20, 52, 53, 80, 83, 87, 90, 91, 93, 110. (See Plumbago.)
Grau-wacke. (See Graywacke.)
Gravel, 13, 33, 34, 35, 50, 90, 96–104.
Gray, 29, 55, 62.
Graywacke, 6, 9–12, 60–63, 91, 96, 104, 107.
Graywacke slate, 61, 63.
Great Pond, 35.
Greenland, 45.
Green Mts., 24, 28, 36.
Greenstone, 9, 59, 93.
Greylock, 57.
Grit, 16, 19, 51.
Grooves. (See Glacial striae.)
Gulf of Maine, 29, 42.
Gull Island, 13.
Gull Rocks, 50.
Gutbier, 69, 73, 75, 76.
Gypsum, 20, 66, 81.

Hagar, 21.
Haldeman, 17.
Hall, 20.
Hanging Rocks, 48, 51, 93.
Harbor Pond, 34.
Harbors, origin of, 26.
Hard-pan, 39, 97, 100, 102, 104. (See Till.)
Harden's, 64.
Hare, 6.

Harris, 65.
Harris ledge, 91. (See Lime Rock.)
Harrisburg, 36, 40.
Hartford, 34.
Harvard, 33.
Harvard College, 44, 52.
Hawes, 30, 106, 111.
Hayes, 15.
Hearth-stones, 88.
Heat, internal, 22.
Hematite, 23, 34, 65, 80, 81, 87, 91, 110.
Herman, 15.
Hickory nuts, 56.
Highest point, 88.
Hill removed, 99.
Hills, 32, 50, 90, 91.
Hills of drift, 13, 14, 34, 38, 45–47, 54, 99.
Hitchcock, C. H., 18–22, 28, 29, 34, 37, 44, 47, 48, 50, 55, 56, 69–78, 106–108.
Hitchcock, E., 10–18, 21, 24, 31, 42, 43, 47, 50, 57, 69, 87, 106, 107.
Hodge, 15.
Hoffman, 69, 71.
Holbrook, 58.
Holley, 34.
Holmes, 21.
Hopkins, 90, 91.
Hopkinton, 67, 85.
Hornblende, 53, 65, 67, 83, 84, 87, 93, 110.
Hornblende gneiss, 87.
Hornblende rock, 9, 24, 41, 42, 59, 65, 90, 108.
Hornblende schist, 37, 51, 57.
Hornblende slate, 11, 12, 61.
Hornstone, 83.
Household Sew. Mach. Co., 98.
Hoyt, 55, 71, 72, 114.
Hudson Bay, 25.
Hudson River, 29.
Hummock, 35.
Hunt, 20, 21, 23–25, 28–30, 36, 37, 50, 53, 57, 106, 108.
Hunt's Mill, 91.
Hunting Hill, 59, 63.
Huronian, 19, 20, 24, 29, 36, 41, 53, 56, 106, 108.
Hutton. (See Lindley.)
Hymenophyllites, 70.
Hypozoic, 2, 17.

Ice, 56. (See Glaciers, Icebergs.)
Icebergs, 25, 52.
Iceberg theory, 13, 27, 47.
Ice caps, polar, 45, 47.
Ice, eroding power of, 30, 36, 45, 46, 47.
Iceland spar, 82.
Ice melting. (See Floods.)

INDEX.   121

Ice melting below 32°, 31.
Ide's ledge, 91.
Igneous rocks, 9, 10, 17, 19, 36, 51, 106, 108, 110. (See Eruptive.)
Illinois, 16, 68, 111.
Ilmenite, 23, 81, 92.
Ilvaite, 4, 85.
Indian Burying Hill, 38.
Indian ledge, 90.
India Point, 99.
Infusorial earth, 83.
Indurated slate, 61, 63.
Indurated talc, 86.
Insect, fossil, 49, 55, 79.
International Geol. Cong., 56.
Iowa, 16.
Ireland, 63.
Iron Mine Hill, 44, 60, 81, 87, 112, 114. (See Cumberland.)
Iron mines, 23, 34, 59, 65-67, 80, 91.
Iron ores, 5, 6, 8, 10-12, 19, 20, 23, 31, 34, 44, 45, 52, 53, 55, 64-67, 80, 81, 87, 94, 100, 112-114. (See Analysis.)
Iron pyrites. (See Pyrite.)
Iron sand, 5, 23, 34, 35, 53, 81, 94, 98.
Iron Trade Review, 55.
Iron vitriol, 81.
Island, floating, 88.

Jackson, C. T., 8, 12, 14, 15, 18, 21.
Jackson's Catalogue, 58-68.
Jackson's R. I. Report, 8-10, 17, 41, 42, 50, 52, 70, 72, 73, 79, 81, 83, 84, 87, 88, 90, 91, 93-95, 105-108.
Jackson, W. M., 97, 98.
Jamestown, 80-86, 94. (See Conanicut.)
Jamestown Ferry, 51.
Jasper, 8, 11, 19, 67, 83, 94.
Jenckes, 60, 68.
Jenkins, 59, 61, 62.
Jenkins' quarry, 90.
Johnson, 12, 107.
Johnston, 9, 41, 59, 61-63, 66-68, 80-86, 89, 100, 108, 111.
Johnston, A. K., 17.
Jointer ledge, 59, 61.
Joints, 12, 19, 21, 93. (See Fissures.)
Joints, theories of, 18, 21, 48, 49.
Journal Acad. Nat. Sci., 4, 6.
Journal Geol. Soc. London, 14, 70.
Journal. (See American, Boston, Manufacturers, Providence.)

Kame rivers, 48.
Kames, 30, 33, 34, 36, 37, 39, 41, 43-46, 53, 54, 56.
Kaolinite, 86.
Kelly, 111.
Kettle-holes, 41.

Kettle Point, 99.
Keweenian, 36.
Kidston, 70.
Kilkenny, 63.
King, 33, 48.
Knebelite, 67, 84, 85, 87.
Knight, 59.
Knight's hotel, 59.
Kyanite, 85.

Labrador, 22, 45.
Labradorian, 24, 29, 36.
Labradorite, 85.
Lake basins, 22, 31, 45, 46.
Land, depression of, 22, 28, 29, 31, 32, 35, 40, 45, 47.
Land, elevation of, 5, 27, 31, 40, 44, 47, 55. (See Level.)
Lantern Hill, 13.
Laurentian, 19, 20, 24, 29, 36, 53, 56, 108.
Laurentide Mts., 20.
Ledges, 34, 40, 46, 54, 59, 61, 87-96, 98-105.
Lenticular hills, 34, 37, 39, 45, 54.
Lepidodendron, 77.
Lepidophyllum, 77, 78.
Lepidostrobus, 77.
Leslie, 33.
Lesquereux, 19, 20, 40, 41, 53, 68-79, 110, 111.
Level, changes of, 29, 42. (See Land.)
Lewis, 28, 35.
Lievrite, 4, 85.
Life, evidence of earliest, 20, 31, 52.
Lignite, 34, 38, 56, 86, 94.
Lime, 88, 90.
Lime, carbonate of. (See Limestone.)
Lime (Rock) Islands, 50, 59, 62, 94.
Lime Rock, 81-86, 88.
Lime Rock, Dexter, 61, 80, 81, 83, 85, 86, 88.
Lime Rock, Harris, 58, 59, 61, 62, 67, 68, 81, 86, 88, 112.
Lime Rock, Middle, 59, 61, 62, 65, 67, 88.
Limestone, 11, 12, 19, 20, 24, 30, 41,- 43, 52, 55, 61, 62, 66-68, 81, 82, 85, 87, 88, 90, 94, 95, 106, 108, 110-113.
Limestone, black, 82.
Limestone, blue, 62, 82.
Limestone breccia, 62.
Limestone, buff, 62.
Limestone, granular, 62, 65, 82, 90.
Limestone, green, 62, 67, 82.
Limestone, yellow, 82.
Limestone. (See Dolomite, Magnesian, Origin, Stratified.)
Limonite, 61, 81, 91. (See Brown Hematite.)

Lincoln, 79-86, 88, 104, 106, 108.
Lindley and Hutton, 69, 75, 76, 78.
Lingula, 18, 26, 31, 43, 48, 51, 79, 108.
Lingulella, 79.
Lippitt, 33, 113.
Little Compton, 10-12, 30, 48, 58, 83.
Livermore, 34.
Localities, interesting, 87-95, 114.
Logan, 20, 21, 53.
London, 14, 17, 37, 70.
Long Island, 2, 13, 14, 23, 26-28, 32, 34-39, 41, 44-46, 49, 50, 53.
Long Island Sound, 13, 31, 92.
Lotteries, 2, 3.
Louisquisset pike, 58, 60, 62, 63.
Lyceum. (See Annals.)
Lycopodiaceæ, 77, 78.
Lydian stone, 83.
Lyell, 13, 14, 27, 107, 110.
Lyman, 22.

Macfarlane, 40.
Mackerel Cove, 94.
Maclure, 3, 107.
Macrostachya, 77.
Magnesia, 23.
Magnesian limestone, 24, 30, 42, 61, 62, 82. (See Dolomite.)
Magnesian rocks, 20.
Magnesian slate, 110.
Magnetic iron ore, 5, 6, 10, 23, 34, 44, 53, 65-67, 81, 112. (See Cumberland iron.)
Magnetic sand. (See Iron sand.)
Magnetite, 10, 34, 44, 65, 66, 81, 87, 90, 92, 93, 95, 114.
Magnetite eruptive, 44.
Magnetite metamorphic, 44.
Maine, 8, 21, 22, 29, 41, 47, 110.
Maine Geol. Reports, 8, 21.
Malachite, 80.
Mammillary chalcedony, 83.
Mammillary hematite, 80.
Mammillary hills, 54.
Man, 61.
Manganese, 7, 23, 66, 81, 82, 88.
Manganese, black oxide, 66, 81.
Manganese, ferro-silicate, 7, 84.
Manganese, silicate, 67, 84.
Mansfield, 16, 63, 64, 69, 71, 73-76, 94.
Manton, 90, 100.
Manufacturers and Farmers Journal, 7, 15.
Manville, 59, 66, 80, 84.
Maps, geological, 3, 9, 11, 12, 14, 17, 18, 21, 28, 29, 40-44, 48-53, 55, 56, 95, 99, 106, 108. (See Coloration.)
Maps, topographical, 33, 55, 57, 109, 113. (See Charts.)

Marble. (See Limestone, granular.)
Marcou, 17, 53.
Marine fossils, 31, 32, 79.
Marl, 66, 102, 104.
Marshes, 113.
Martha's Vineyard, 33, 37, 39, 45.
Mashapaug Pond, 103.
Mason, 7, 62, 64.
Masonite, 12, 14, 15, 68, 86, 91.
Massachusetts, 3, 8, 10-12, 15-17, 23, 30, 36, 41-43, 54, 55, 57, 94, 95, 107, 109, 110, 112.
Massachusetts Bay, 40.
Massachusetts, Eastern, Geol. of, 30, 36, 41-43.
Massachusetts Geol. Reports, 10-12, 15, 16, 30, 69.
Massachusetts Top. Survey, 55, 57, 109.
Mather, 8, 13.
McGee, 55.
Meade, 3, 4, 7.
Medical Repository, 109.
Medical topography, 40.
Melanterite, 81.
Memoirs Boston Soc. Nat. Hist., 22, 29.
Menaccanite, 81, 90, 92.
Merrill, 92, 111.
Merrimack Valley, 33, 36.
Mesozoic, 106.
Messages, Governors', 33, 55, 57.
Metamorphic coal, 12, 16, 17, 110. (See Anthracite.)
Metamorphic grit, 51.
Metamorphic iron ore, 44.
Metamorphic rocks, 2, 10, 17, 19, 28, 52, 60-62, 106, 108.
Metamorphic slates, 11, 12, 42, 63.
Metamorphism, 16, 20-22, 27, 37, 42, 44, 52, 92, 108.
Metasomatosis, 37.
Miantonomah Hill, 19, 50, 63, 94.
Mica, 51, 58, 60, 67, 85, 88, 92, 93.
Micaceous iron, 80, 90.
Mica schist, 20, 21, 37, 44, 51, 52, 85, 91.
Mica slate, 6, 9, 11, 12, 17, 42, 60, 63, 67, 88, 90.
Michigan, 16.
Microcline, 85.
Microscopic structure, 30, 44, 92, 106, 114.
Middletown, 11, 12, 70, 76, 78, 81-86, 93.
Mill River, 32.
Millstone Grit, 16, 19, 43, 107.
Mineralogical Journal, 3.
Mineralogy, works on, 3, 6, 8, 14, 35.
Minerals, catalogues of, 6, 30, 65-68, 79-86, 114.

Minerals, localities of, 4-7, 61-68, 79-95.
Minerals of R. I., study of, 105.
Mineral springs, 90, 91, 113.
Mine-holes, 81, 87.
Mines. (See Coal and Iron,)
Mispickel, 80.
Mistissinny Lake, 25.
Mitchell, 109.
Modern Petrography, 106.
Molybdenite, 80, 87.
Molybdenum sulphide, 5, 65, 80.
Money stone, 92.
Montalban, 24, 29, 36, 41, 42, 53, 108.
Montauk Point, 14, 37, 38.
Moshassuck River, 88.
Moraines, 13, 43, 45-47.
Moraines, ground, 38, 39, 97.
Moraines, intermediate, 46, 47, 92.
Moraines, lateral, 28.
Moraines, terminal, 25, 26, 28, 30, 33, 35-39, 44-49, 53, 92, 94, 109.
Mountain leather, 84.
Mount Hope, 11, 41, 58, 66, 82, 93.
Mount Hope Coal Mine, 15.
Mount Pleasant, 40, 90, 100.
Mud, 99, 101, 103.
Muscovite, 85, 94.
Museum Comp. Zoöl., 44, 52.
Mylacris, 55, 79.

Nacrite, 7, 85, 88.
Nail-head spar, 62, 82.
Nantucket, 37, 39.
Narragansett basin, 42, 43, 68, 113.
Narragansett Bay, 9, 13, 16, 25-27, 30-33, 42, 45, 47, 48, 50-52, 55, 57, 81, 106, 107, 109.
Narragansett Park, 103.
Narragansett Pier, 50, 51, 81, 104.
Natick, 60, 67, 68, 84, 86, 91.
National Atlas, 55.
National Rubber Co., 104.
Natural faces, 88, 91.
Natural Hist., Boston Journ. of, 14, 69, 110.
Natural Hist., N. Y., 13, 110.
Naushon, 33.
Nayatt Brick Co., 104.
Neck, Block Island, 35.
Negley, 113.
Nephrite, 4, 6, 30, 67, 86, 110.
Neptunian, 37.
Neuropteris, 69-71.
Neutakonkanut Hill, 59, 60, 66, 90, 100.
Newberry, 47, 69, 72.
New England, 2, 8, 11, 17, 19, 22, 24, 25, 27-32, 36, 37, 39-41, 43, 44, 46-49, 53, 57, 87.
New England Coal Mining Co., 8.
Newfoundland, 24.

New Hampshire, 14, 29, 30, 34, 36.
New Hampshire Geol. Reports, 14, 29, 30, 106, 109.
New Haven, 8, 12, 14, 25, 27, 31, 32, 49.
New Jersey, 7, 36, 37, 45, 49.
Newport, 3, 5, 6, 10-12, 16, 18, 19, 21, 23, 24, 29-31, 36, 41-43, 48-52, 57, 59, 61-65, 78-86, 93, 94, 104, 106, 108, 109, 111, 112, 114.
Newport Neck, 19, 50-52, 59, 61, 64-67, 81, 86, 94, 106.
Newportite, 86.
Newport Nat. Hist. Soc. (See Proceedings.)
New species, fossil, 69, 70, 72, 79, 114.
New survey, need of, 9, 33, 55-57, 105, 106, 109, 113.
New York, 4-8, 13, 15, 17, 21, 32, 44, 58, 110.
New York Carbon Iron Co., 113.
New York Geol. Reports, 13, 14, 110, 111.
New York Medical Repository, 109.
New York Tribune, 113.
Niantic, 111.
Nicholson File Co., 101, 102.
Niles, 23.
Nipmuck quarry, 60, 94, 112.
Noeggerathia, 75.
No Man's Land, 37, 39.
Nomenclature, 56.
Norfolk County basin, 30, 43.
Norian, 24, 36, 53.
North Adams, 57.
North America, 47, 53.
North American Review, 30.
North Carolina, 17.
North Kingstown, 50, 60, 63, 86, 92.
North Providence, 7, 59-63, 68, 79, 82-84, 86, 94, 95.
North Sandwich, 37.
North Smithfield, 79, 81-83, 86, 88.
Nova Scotia, 20.

Obliteration of fossils, 108.
Ocean, 5, 20, 22.
Ocean, depression of, 22, 27, 40. (See Land.)
Ochre, 63, 65, 80, 81, 94.
Octahedrite, 80.
Odontopteris, 72.
Ohio, 16.
Old Mountain, 38.
Old Red Sandstone, 11, 107, 110.
Olivine, 37, 44, 84, 87, 114.
Opal, 83.
Opinion, changes of, 106.
Orange County, N. Y., 44.
Ordovician, 106, 112.

Orient Point, 37.
Origin of crystalline rocks, 20, 21, 24, 25, 36, 37, 57, 108.
Origin of limestones and dolomite, 12, 20, 24, 108.
Origin of silicates, 20, 37.
Orthoclase, 85, 92.
Ottrelite, 52, 86, 94.

Packard, 22, 27, 56.
Packard's Rocks, 50.
Palæophycus, 79.
Paleozoic, 19, 20, 24, 30, 36, 37, 42, 52, 79, 107, 109, 112.
Pallasite, 114.
Paradise, 19, 26, 48, 49, 51, 56, 85, 86, 93.
Parallel drift hills, 54.
Parallel ridges, 23, 54.
Parsons, 40.
Partridge, 5.
Pascoag gneiss, 94, 111.
Pawtucket, 9-12, 63, 71, 79, 81-83, 86, 94, 112, 114.
Pawtuxet, 80, 82, 83, 86.
Pearl spar, 82, 83.
Peat, 34, 35, 54, 56, 64, 94.
Pebbles, 10, 13, 18, 19, 21, 22, 26, 27, 29, 31, 33, 38, 42, 43, 45, 48, 52, 54, 63, 92, 93, 98, 101, 108.
Pebbles, elongated. (See Purgatory.)
Pecopteris, 68, 69, 72-74.
Peirce, 25, 30.
Pennsylvania, 3, 7, 12, 14, 16, 17, 20, 36, 40, 107, 111.
Pennsylvania Geol. Reports, 36, 40, 41, 68-79, 111.
Percival, 12.
Peridotyte, 44, 81.
Perry, 27, 114.
Perryville, 38.
Petrography, Modern, 106.
Petrosilex, 37.
Philadelphia, 3-6, 12, 17, 21, 29, 40, 55.
Phillips, 14, 58.
Phosphorus, 23.
Photicite, 84, 87.
Phyllite, 86, 90, 91, 104.
Picrolite, 86, 88, 94.
Pine cones, 56.
Pinnularia, 78.
Pittsburg, 113.
Plagioclase, 44, 85, 114.
Plains, 14, 30, 35.
Planes of division. (See Joints.)
Plasticity, 18, 19, 21, 22, 31, 93.
Plications, 49.
Plumbaginous anthracite, 28, 52.
Plumbaginous argillyte, 52.
Plumbago, 6, 14, 19, 20, 28, 52, 53, 64, 80, 91, 96, 102. (See Graphite.)

Plum Island, 13, 37, 39, 41.
Plutonic rocks, 36.
Plymouth County, 16, 42.
Pocasset Coal and Iron Co., 23.
Point Judith, 31, 32, 38, 39, 41, 47, 50, 58.
Poker Hill, 80.
Pomp's Pond, 43.
Pond filled, 99.
Ponds, 25, 34, 35, 38, 40.
Poppasquash Neck, 63, 64, 92.
Popular Science Monthly, 28, 35, 44.
Porphyritic gneiss, 60.
Porphyritic granite, 58-60.
Porphyritic magnetite, 53, 66, 81, 87.
Porphyry, 12, 17, 26.
Port Jefferson, 37, 39.
Portsmouth, 3, 10-12, 16, 17, 19, 23, 30, 34, 54, 57, 63, 64, 74, 80-82, 84, 86, 93.
Portsmouth Coal, 3, 16, 17, 19, 34, 54, 57, 63, 64.
Portsmouth mines, 3, 23, 64, 93.
Post-Tertiary, 25, 27, 36.
Pot-holes, 15.
Potsdam, 18, 79, 106, 112.
Potter's, 65.
Potter's Hill, 67.
Powell, 46, 55.
Prang Ed. Co., 114.
Prase, 67, 82, 87.
Presl, 78.
Pre-glacial sand hills, 32.
Price's Neck, 61.
Primary rocks, 2, 9, 10, 13, 17, 60-62, 108, 110.
Prime, 40, 112.
Primitive rocks, 2, 3, 7, 108.
Primordial, 42, 43, 53, 106.
Proceedings Acad. Nat. Sci., 12.
Proceedings Amer. Assoc. Adv. Sci., 15, 18, 22, 24, 28, 34, 36, 39, 41, 47, 48, 69.
Proceedings Boston Soc. Nat. Hist., 15, 18, 22, 23, 27, 30, 31, 33, 34, 37, 41, 45, 48, 51, 56, 114.
Proceedings Canad. Inst., 22.
Proceedings Newport Nat. Hist. Soc., 48, 49, 51, 52, 69, 114.
Prospect Hill, 7, 90.
Protogine, 19, 51, 58.
Providence, 2-8, 11, 15, 16, 19, 22, 23, 31-33, 40, 42, 53, 55, 58, 63-65, 71, 79, 80-86, 88-92, 94-103, 111, 112, 114.
Providence Gas Co., 103.
Providence Journal, 23, 24, 40, 53, 55-57, 112, 113.
Providence Press, 47.
Providence River, 99.
Providence Steam Engine Co., 99.

INDEX. 125

Providence Worsted Mills, 102.
Prudence Island, 93.
Pseudomorphism, 20, 83, 86, 94.
Pseudopecopteris, 74, 75.
Publications, 2-57, 109-116.
Pudding stone, 22. (See Conglom.)
Pumpelly, 112.
Purgatory, 6, 10-12, 15, 19, 22, 31, 48-51, 63, 93. (See Distortion.)
Putnam, 54.
Pyrite, 8, 64-66, 79-81, 83, 88, 92, 94, 104.
Pyrolusite, 81, 87.
Pyroxene, 20, 84.

Quarries, 87-92, 94, 95, 111, 112.
Quartz, 7, 20, 43, 53, 65-67, 81-83, 85, 87, 92, 93, 98, 103, 104, 110.
Quartz, blue, 82.
Quartz, cellular, 83.
Quartz crystals, 53, 66, 80, 82, 83, 88, 93.
Quartz, drusy, 66, 82.
Quartz, ferruginous, 83.
Quartz, fetid, 83.
Quartz, fibrous, 83.
Quartz, granular, 61, 66, 83, 88.
Quartz, greasy, 82.
Quartzite, 20, 42, 48, 52.
Quartz, massive, 83.
Quartz, milky, 66, 82, 91, 93.
Quartz, opalized, 83.
Quartzose aggregates, 11.
Quartz pebbles, 63.
Quartz, pseudomorphous, 83.
Quartz, radiated, 83.
Quartz rock, 12, 59, 66, 110.
Quartz, rose, 82.
Quartz, sagenitic, 67, 83, 93.
Quartz, smoky, 66.
Quartz, stalactitic, 83, 88.
Quartz veins, origin of, 110.
Quartzyte conglomerate, 51.
Quaternary, 25, 47.
Quick-sand, 98-104.
Quincy granite, 41.
Quinnipiac River, 32.

Rachiopteris, 75.
Railway demand for topographic maps, 113.
Random Notes Nat. Hist., 49, 53, 55, 56.
Ravines, 56, 91. (See Valleys.)
Razy, 58, 60, 63.
Reclamation of marshes, 113.
Red chalk, 80.
Red graywacke, 63.
Red ochre, 80.
Reform School, 103.
Reindeer, 31.
Remarks, general, 105-109.

Report, U. S. Coast Survey, 25-27.
Reports, geolog. and topograph.
  Amer. Geog. Soc., 32.
  Canada, 21, 53.
  Conn., 8, 12, 13.
  Ills., 68, 111.
  Maine, 8, 21.
  Mass., 10-12, 15, 16, 30, 55, 69. (See Massachusetts.)
  N. H., 14, 29, 30, 106, 109.
  N. J., 36.
  N. Y., 13, 14, 110, 111.
  Penn., 36, 40, 41, 68-79, 111.
  R. I., 8-10, 15, 23, 25-27, 33, 40, 58-68, 113. (See Jackson's, Governors'.)
  U. S., 46, 47, 55, 112, 113. (See Bulletin.)
  Vt., 14, 21.
  (See Surveys.)
Rhabdocarpus, 78.
Rhacophyllum, 70, 75.
Rhode Island, island of. (See Aquidneck.)
Rhode Island American, 3.
Rhode Island Citizen, 53.
Rhode Island Coal Co., 3.
Rhode Island Tool Co., 100.
Rhodonite, 84.
Rhomb spar, 62, 82, 88.
Ribbon agate, 83.
Richmond, 58, 60.
Richmond Mfg. Co., 102.
Ridges, 30, 33. (See Paradise, Snake Den, Wolf Rocks.)
Ridgeway, 22, 23.
River Point, 104.
Rivers, erosion by, 17.
River-valley formations, 31, 32.
Robinson, 5-7, 79, 81, 94.
Roches moutonnées, 26.
Rock basins, 46.
Rock crystal, 82.
Rock, decaying, 89.
Rock Farm, 61, 65.
Rocking stones, 5, 7, 91, 94.
Rockland factories, 58, 60.
Rocks of R. I., lists of, 11, 12, 58-64, 114.
Rocks of R. I., study of, 106-109.
Rocks, unstratified, 58, 59. (See Igneous.)
Rocky Hill, 100.
Rocky Mts., 33.
Roehl, 71.
Roemer, 69, 72.
Rogers, H. D., 17, 20, 111.
Rogers, W. B., 18, 21, 31, 79, 93.
Roger Williams Rock, 96, 99.
Rose Island, 50, 86.

Rose quartz, 82.
Round Rocks, 53, 89.
Rumstick Point, 63.
Rutile, 80, 83, 90, 92, 93.

Sachuest, 48, 51, 93.
Sachuest Point, 19, 30, 76.
Sagenite. (See Quartz.)
Sahlite, 67, 84.
Saint John's Church, 88.
Saint Lawrence River, 25.
Saint Lawrence Co., N. Y., 110.
Saint Stephen's Church, 88, 112.
Salisbury, 45, 69, 75, 78, 114.
Sand, 5, 13, 26, 34, 35, 39, 50, 53, 54, 64, 81, 90, 94, 96-104. (See Iron.)
Sand, absence of, 26.
Sand-drifts, 93.
Sand Hill, 38.
Sands' Pond, 35.
Sandstone, 14, 16, 19, 43, 103, 107.
Sandy Hill, 35, 56.
Sandy Point, 35, 48.
Sankaty Head, 37.
Saussurite, 85, 110.
Sayles' Bleachery, 80.
Saylesville, 104.
Schimper, 69, 72, 75, 76.
Schist, 19, 20, 51. (See Hornblende, Mica.)
Schlotheim, 69, 72, 73, 75.
Science, 47, 48, 57, 109, 112, 113.
Science Advocate, 45.
Scientific work, U. S., 55.
Scituate, 58, 60, 80-82, 84, 85, 94.
Scolithus, 43, 79.
Scoria, 61.
Scotland, 16.
Scott's Pond, 88.
Scratches. (See Glacial striae.)
Scudder, 30, 55, 69, 114.
Scythe-stones, 60, 88.
Sea-border formations, 31.
Sea level. (See Land.)
Sea salt, origin of, 20.
Secondary rocks, 3, 17.
Sections, geological, 9, 17, 19, 25, 45, 48, 50, 51, 87, 88, 90, 93, 94, 110.
Sections. (See Microscopic.)
Seeds, fossil, 78.
Seekonk, 11, 16, 47, 54, 63, 81, 86.
Seekonk River, 97, 99.
Separation of minerals, 106.
Serpentine, 12, 15, 19, 20, 23, 29, 37, 44, 59, 60, 66, 86, 88, 90, 94, 109, 110, 114.
Serpentine rock, 59.
Sewage works, 103.
Sewage drawn to well, 103.
Shale, 43, 96, 102, 104.
Shaler, 22, 23, 25-27, 29, 30, 45, 50, 55, 106, 108, 109, 111, 113.

Shawmut group, 42, 106.
Shepard, 5, 7, 8,
Shells, 98, 99.
Shock and Ice, 26, 45.
Shore in Carbonif. times, 26, 50.
Shurrocks, 114.
Siderite, 61, 81, 83, 90, 93, 94.
Sideritic argillyte, 51, 61.
Sigillaria, 43, 78.
Silex, 110.
Silicates, origin of, 20.
Siliceous argillyte, 51, 106.
Siliceous rocks, 111.
Siliceous slate, 19.
Silliman, 4, 6, 7, 10.
Silliman's Journal, 15. (See Amer. Journ. Science.)
Silurian, 10, 24, 26, 28, 29, 36, 43, 51, 55, 56, 79, 106, 108, 112.
Silver, 2, 80. (See Argentiferous.)
Silver Spring, 91, 99, 103.
Silver Spring Co., 100, 101.
Slate, 4, 9, 16, 18-20, 30, 41-43, 51, 52, 60-66, 84, 96, 98, 99, 102-104.
Slate Hill, 63.
Slickensides, 45, 49.
Smith, 15.
Smithfield, 4-7, 9, 11, 12, 30, 41, 53, 58-62, 65-68, 79, 81, 82, 84, 85, 110-112.
Smithfield granite, 111, 112.
Smithfield Granite Co., 111.
Smithfield ledge, 88.
Smithfield limestone stratified, 110.
Smith's Hill, 90, 100.
Smithsonian, 17, 29.
Smithtown, 14.
Snock, 36, 48.
Snake Den, 89, 111.
Sneech Pond, 87.
Soapstone, 59, 86, 90. (See Steatite.)
Soapstone rock, 68.
Society Enc. Domes. Indus., 9, 23.
Sockanosset, 64, 91, 103.
Soda carbonate, 20.
Soils, 9, 34, 64, 89, 110.
Soundings, 55, 57, 99, 101.
Southgate, 60.
South Kingstown, 38, 39, 50, 58, 60, 85, 86, 91, 92.
South Kingstown Ferry, 60.
South Scituate, 94.
Sow-backs, 54.
Spathic iron, 81.
Specular iron, 80.
Specular schist, 20.
Sphene, 86, 92.
Sphenophyllum, 69, 76, 77.
Sphenopteris, 68-70, 74, 75.
Spinelle, 110.
Springfield Repub., 113.
Springs, 35, 90, 91, 97, 113.

INDEX.

Stalactitic hematite, 65, 80.
Stalactitic quartz, 83, 88.
Starve-goat Island, 103.
Statistics of coal, 17, 112.
Staurolite, 28, 52, 86, 94.
Staurotide, 86.
Steatite, 20, 81, 84, 86-88, 90. (See Soapstone.)
Steel, 113.
Sternberg, 69, 71, 75-78.
Stigmaria, 69, 78.
Stilbite, 86.
Stockbridge limestone, 110.
Stone, 41, 48.
Stone. (See Building.)
Strata, 11, 19, 53, 54, 57, 95-105, 113..
Strata, age of R. I., 106-109.
Stratified limestone, 42, 110.
Stratified primary rocks, 60-62.
Striae. (See Glacial.)
Strike, 11, 16, 19, 41, 48, 50.
Sub-carboniferous, 19, 43, 107, 108, 111.
Submarine channels, 40, 44.
Substitution, 64.
Sulphur, 23, 52, 79.
Sulphurets, 20.
Surface geology, 2, 17, 20, 36, 109.
Surface rock. (See Ledges.)
Survey. (See New.)
Surveys, geological, 30, 33, 40, 105, 106, 113. (See Reports.)
Surveys, topographical, 30, 32, 33, 55-57, 105, 109, 113. (See Coast Survey.)
Swanzey, 62, 63.
Syenite, 12, 17, 24, 26, 59, 87, 111.

Taberg, 44.
Taconian, 36, 53.
Taconic, 17, 106, 108, 110, 112.
Taggart's Ferry, 48.
Talc, 5, 59, 62. 68, 86, 88, 90, 93, 94, 110.
Talco-micaceous slate, 60, 61.
Talcose limestone, 62.
Talcose rock, 59, 66.
Talcose schist, 18, 20, 21.
Talcose slate, 12, 61, 65.
Taunton, 43.
Taunton River, 10.
Taylor, 5, 17, 83.
Temiscamang Lake, 25.
Terrace formation, 36, 44.
Terraces, 13, 15, 28, 30-32, 45.
Terranovan, 24, 36.
Tertiary, 9, 13, 28, 32, 33, 39, 50, 64, 107.
Teschemacher, 14, 68-74, 76.
Test wells, 99, 101, 103.
Text-books, 2, 4, 21, 35.

Theories. (See Crenitic, Distortion, Drift, Glacial, Iceberg, Joints, Origin.)
Thetis hair stone, 83, 87.
Thomson, 7.
Thurber, 94.
Thurber's ledge, 90, 111.
Thurston, 23.
Till, 30, 38, 39, 44, 46, 54, 97. (See Hard-pan.)
Titanic hematite, 81.
Titaniferous magnetite, 12, 23, 66, 81, 87, 114.
Titanite, 86.
Titanium, 4.
Titanium oxide, 80.
Tiverton, 10, 11, 19, 41, 50.
Tool Co., 98, 100, 101.
Topaz, false, 82.
Topographical. (See Maps, Surveys.)
Topography, 25, 36. (See Medical.)
Topography of glaciated regions. 45.
Toronto, 52.
Torpedo Station, 104.
Torrey, 5.
Totten, 61.
Tottenite, 61.
Touchstone, 83.
Tourmaline, 85.
Tower Hill, 5, 50, 59, 64, 84, 85, 87, 91.
Trade, Board of, 113.
Transactions Amer. Inst. Mining Eng., 34, 40, 54, 56.
Transactions Amer. Phil. Soc., 5.
Transactions, Assoc. Amer. Geol., 12, 13.
Transition formation, 3, 4, 7, 9, 10, 17, 107.
Transition graywacke, 62, 107.
Transportation of drift, 10, 12, 13, 26, 27, 54, 56, 81, 87, 89-91. (See Glacial motion, Cumberland iron boulders.)
Trap rock, 9, 10, 13, 31, 36, 59, 93, 110.
Travertine, 82.
Trees, Block Is., 34, 35, 56.
Tremolite, 7, 67, 84, 87, 88.
Triassic, 43, 107.
Trilobite, 114.
Troost, 4, 5.
Troy, 10.
Tucker, 95.
Tucker's Pond, 39.

Unger, 78.
United States Geol. Survey, 46, 47, 53, 55-57, 108, 112, 113.
United States scientific work, 55.

Upham, 29, 34, 36–40, 46, 48, 109.
Uxbridge, 65.

Valenciennes, 70.
Valley Falls, 16, 19, 80, 86, 87.
Valley Falls mine, 87.
Valley Worsted Co., 102.
Valleys, 14, 25, 31, 35, 36, 39, 46, 47, 49, 51, 89. (See Glacial depressions.)
Valleys, pre-glacial, 46, 56.
Value of topog. maps, 32, 109, 114.
Vanuxem, 6, 17.
Veins, dislocated, 49.
Veins of basalt, 6.
Veins of quartz, origin, 110.
Vermont, 14, 17, 18, 21, 110.
Vermont Geol. Reports, 14, 21.
Village Hill, 38.
Virginia, 16.
Vitriol works, 101.
Volkmannia, 77.
Vose, 22.

Wadsworth, 44, 52, 114.
Wakefield, 38.
Walcott, 112.
Walker, 28, 55.
Walling, 55.
Wallum Pond, 95.
Warren, 11, 62, 63.
Warren's Point, 58.
Warwick, 5, 9, 11, 12, 19, 58, 60, 68, 73, 74, 80, 81, 83, 86, 91.
Warwick Neck, 58, 64, 91, 104.
Washington, 55, 113.
Washington Bridge, 99.
Watch Hill, 31, 32.
Water in coal, 54, 93.
Water supply, 97–105.
Waterman quarry, 111.
Watertown, 23.
Watson's Pier, 85.
Webb, 4, 5, 79, 81, 83, 86.
Webster, 4.

Weight of ice cause depression of land, 44.
Weiss, 74.
Wells, 53, 57, 81, 95, 97–105.
Wernerian, 10.
Westerly, 8, 38, 80–86, 92, 111.
West Island, 50, 51.
West Greenwich, 60, 111.
Wetmore, 57.
Whalebacks, 54.
What Cheer Brewery, 103.
Whelden's ledge, 95.
Whetstones, 88.
Whipple, 59, 61, 62, 66.
White, 59, 65–67.
White Mountains, 24, 36.
Whiting, 55.
Whitney, 15, 30, 52.
Whittlesey, 22.
Wickford, 11, 12, 47, 60, 86, 94.
Wilkesbarre, 74.
Williams, 88, 96, 106.
Williamstown, 57.
Willow Grove, 59, 61.
Wilson, 33.
Windmill Hill, 100.
Wolf Rocks, 56, 91.
Wood's Castle, 48, 93.
Woonasquatucket River, 101, 102.
Woonsocket, 6, 60, 79–81, 84–86, 88, 111, 112.
Woonsocket Falls, 60.
Woonsocket Hill, 61, 66, 83, 88.
Worcester, 10, 14, 21.
Worden's Pond, 39.
Wrentham, 16, 19, 63, 64, 77, 94.
Wright, 33, 37, 41, 43, 47, 53.

Yale College, 4.
Yellow ochre, 63, 65, 81, 94.
Yenite, 4–7, 85, 87.

Zeiller, 70.
Zoisite, 5, 6, 11, 12, 67, 85, 93.

ADDENDA.
(Not included in Index.)

1876. JAMES T. GARDNER. "Relation between Topographical Surveys and the Study of Public Health." An address delivered before the American Public Health Association, at Boston. 10 pp., Albany.

1884. M. E. WADSWORTH. *Memoirs of the Museum of Comparative Zoölogy* at Harvard College, in Cambridge, vol. 11, "Lithological Studies," Part I., pp. 75-83. The "Cumberlandite" of Iron Mine Hill, Cumberland, an apparently eruptive mass of magnetite, containing crystals of olivine, feldspar, etc., is described as a terrestrial variety of Pallasite. On plates 1 and 2, figures are given of microscopic sections of the rock. See pp. 44 and 114 of this Report.

1886. H. F. WALLING. "Topographic Surveys of States." Read before the Boston Society of Civil Engineers, pp. 163-176.

1888. *Providence Journal.* "Advantages of a State Geological Survey," an editorial article, Feb. 1.

Report of Meeting of "R. I. Historical Society. Advantages of a Topographical and Geological Survey of the State Advocated." Papers by A. S. Packard and S. F. Peckham, the former printed nearly in full, Feb. 9.

"Sewer Test Wells. Interesting Conditions Met in Sinking Land and Water Soundings," Feb. 12.

Nearly 200 test wells have been sunk along the lines of the proposed sewers and sewage works at Field's Point and in various parts of the city of Providence, of which accurate records have been kept in the office of the city engineer. The deepest well was nearly 109 feet below high water, on the line of the siphon across the Providence river, from India street to near the foot of Langley street. The depth below high water at which bed-rock was struck on the line of this siphon varies from 89 feet near the east side to 109 feet on the west side, passing through about 19 feet of water, 22 feet of river mud and silt, then layers of sand and fine gravel, very fine sand, and sand and coarse gravel. In India street, near the river, rock was struck at a depth of 96½ feet. At Field's Point, a ledge or boulder was struck at 62 feet depth; but no other ledge was found in that region, even at 96 feet. Between Mill street and the river, just north of the Cleveland Mill, slate ledge was struck at about 16 feet, and on Bark street the rock was from 5 feet to 11 feet, below the surface. Quick-sand was found from Ashburton street to the Wanskuck Mills, at about 10 feet below the surface, and extended as deep as the wells were driven, in one well to a depth of 59 feet. Some quick-sand and very fine sand were also found in other parts of the city, but the materials were mostly coarser sand and gravel. The gravel was more extensive and compact on the east side than on the west side of the river. Very little clay was found. At the corner of Cove and Mathewson streets, was a stratum of river mud or silt. At Field's Point, bog mud and peat were found near the clam house and near the location of the precipitation tanks; and in this region, unlike that of the siphon, the arrangement of the material varied considerably in different wells, even when not more than one or two hundred feet apart.

On Fountain street, near Dean street, Providence, private parties have recently bored 182 feet deep, striking the ledge, overlaid by gravel, at 130 feet from the surface. They went through 52 feet of carboniferous shale, the last part quite black and soft.

Rev. Edgar F. Clark has recently found, at Pawtucket, other rare fossils, one of which is the wing of an insect, closely related to the *Mylacris Packardii*, and much more perfectly preserved than the specimen figured in this Report.

PROVIDENCE, February, 1888.

www.ingramcontent.com/pod-product-compliance
Lightning Source LLC
Chambersburg PA
CBHW030401170426
43202CB00010B/1447